Variables and Patterns

Focus on Algebra

Glenda Lappan, Elizabeth Difanis Phillips,
James T. Fey, Susan N. Friel

Pearson

Boston, Massachusetts

Connected Mathematics® was developed at Michigan State University with financial support from the Michigan State University Office of the Provost, Computing and Technology, and the College of Natural Science.

This material is based upon work supported by the National Science Foundation under Grant No. MDR 9150217 and Grant No. ESI 9986372. Opinions expressed are those of the authors and not necessarily those of the Foundation.

As with prior editions of this work, the authors and administration of Michigan State University preserve a tradition of devoting royalties from this publication to support activities sponsored by the MSU Mathematics Education Enrichment Fund.

Acknowledgments appear on page 130, which constitutes an extension of this copyright page.

13-digit ISBN 978-0-328-90043-5
10-digit ISBN 0-328-90043-5
2 17

A Team of Experts

Glenda Lappan is a University Distinguished Professor in the Program in Mathematics Education (PRIME) and the Department of Mathematics at Michigan State University. Her research and development interests are in the connected areas of students' learning of mathematics and mathematics teachers' professional growth and change related to the development and enactment of K–12 curriculum materials.

Elizabeth Difanis Phillips is a Senior Academic Specialist in the Program in Mathematics Education (PRIME) and the Department of Mathematics at Michigan State University. She is interested in teaching and learning mathematics for both teachers and students. These interests have led to curriculum and professional development projects at the middle school and high school levels, as well as projects related to the teaching and learning of algebra across the grades.

James T. Fey is a Professor Emeritus at the University of Maryland. His consistent professional interest has been development and research focused on curriculum materials that engage middle and high school students in problem-based collaborative investigations of mathematical ideas and their applications.

Susan N. Friel is a Professor of Mathematics Education in the School of Education at the University of North Carolina at Chapel Hill. Her research interests focus on statistics education for middle-grade students and, more broadly, on teachers' professional development and growth in teaching mathematics K–8.

With... Yvonne Grant and Jacqueline Stewart

Yvonne Grant teaches mathematics at Portland Middle School in Portland, Michigan. Jacqueline Stewart is a recently retired high school teacher of mathematics at Okemos High School in Okemos, Michigan. Both Yvonne and Jacqueline have worked on a variety of activities related to the development, implementation, and professional development of the CMP curriculum since its beginning in 1991.

Development Team

CMP3 Authors

Glenda Lappan, University Distinguished Professor, Michigan State University
Elizabeth Difanis Phillips, Senior Academic Specialist, Michigan State University
James T. Fey, Professor Emeritus, University of Maryland
Susan N. Friel, Professor, University of North Carolina – Chapel Hill

With...

Yvonne Grant, Portland Middle School, Michigan
Jacqueline Stewart, Mathematics Consultant, Mason, Michigan

In Memory of... William M. Fitzgerald, Professor (Deceased), Michigan State University, who made substantial contributions to conceptualizing and creating CMP1.

Administrative Assistant

Michigan State University
Judith Martus Miller

Support Staff

Michigan State University
Undergraduate Assistants:
Bradley Robert Corlett, Carly Fleming, Erin Lucian, Scooter Nowak

Development Assistants

Michigan State University
Graduate Research Assistants:
Richard "Abe" Edwards, Nic Gilbertson, Funda Gonulates, Aladar Horvath, Eun Mi Kim, Kevin Lawrence, Jennifer Nimtz, Joanne Philhower, Sasha Wang

Assessment Team

Maine
Falmouth Public Schools
Falmouth Middle School: Shawn Towle

Michigan
Ann Arbor Public Schools
Tappan Middle School
Anne Marie Nicoll-Turner

Portland Public Schools
Portland Middle School
Holly DeRosia, Yvonne Grant

Traverse City Area Public Schools
Traverse City East Middle School
Jane Porath, Mary Beth Schmitt

Traverse City West Middle School
Jennifer Rundio, Karrie Tufts

Ohio
Clark-Shawnee Local Schools
Rockway Middle School: Jim Mamer

Content Consultants

Michigan State University
Peter Lappan, Professor Emeritus, Department of Mathematics

Normandale Community College
Christopher Danielson, Instructor, Department of Mathematics & Statistics

University of North Carolina – Wilmington
Dargan Frierson, Jr., Professor, Department of Mathematics & Statistics

Student Activities

Michigan State University
Brin Keller, Associate Professor, Department of Mathematics

Consultants

Indiana
Purdue University
Mary Bouck, Mathematics Consultant

Michigan
Oakland Schools
Valerie Mills, Mathematics Education
Supervisor
Mathematics Education Consultants:
Geraldine Devine, Dana Gosen

Ellen Bacon, Independent Mathematics
Consultant

New York
University of Rochester
Jeffrey Choppin, Associate Professor

Ohio
University of Toledo
Debra Johanning, Associate Professor

Pennsylvania
University of Pittsburgh
Margaret Smith, Professor

Texas
University of Texas at Austin
Emma Trevino, Supervisor of
Mathematics Programs, The Dana Center

Mathematics for All Consulting
Carmen Whitman, Mathematics Consultant

....

Reviewers

Michigan
Ionia Public Schools
Kathy Dole, Director of Curriculum
and Instruction

Grand Valley State University
Lisa Kasmer, Assistant Professor

Portland Public Schools
Teri Keusch, Classroom Teacher

Minnesota
Hopkins School District 270
Michele Luke, Mathematics Coordinator

....

Field Test Sites for CMP3

Michigan
Ann Arbor Public Schools
Tappan Middle School
Anne Marie Nicoll-Turner*

Portland Public Schools
Portland Middle School: Mark Braun,
Angela Buckland, Holly DeRosia,
Holly Feldpausch, Angela Foote,
Yvonne Grant*, Kristin Roberts,
Angie Stump, Tammi Wardwell

Traverse City Area Public Schools
Traverse City East Middle School
Ivanka Baic Berkshire, Brenda Dunscombe,
Tracie Herzberg, Deb Larimer, Jan Palkowski,
Rebecca Perreault, Jane Porath*,
Robert Sagan, Mary Beth Schmitt*

Traverse City West Middle School
Pamela Alfieri, Jennifer Rundio,
Maria Taplin, Karrie Tufts*

Maine
Falmouth Public Schools
Falmouth Middle School: Sally Bennett,
Chris Driscoll, Sara Jones, Shawn Towle*

Minnesota
Minneapolis Public Schools
Jefferson Community School
Leif Carlson*,
Katrina Hayek Munsisoumang*

Ohio
Clark-Shawnee Local Schools
Reid School: Joanne Gilley
Rockway Middle School: Jim Mamer*
Possum School: Tami Thomas

*Indicates a Field Test Site Coordinator

Variables and Patterns

Focus on Algebra

Looking Ahead

At different times of the year, the number of hours of daylight changes each day. **How** does the number of daylight hours change with the passage of time in a year? **Why** does this happen?

How much should a bike tour company charge each customer in order to make a profit?

• How do you think our tour income will be related to our tour price?
• What price should we charge?
• How do we justify our decision?

Cut back Expenses!

The group admission price for Wild World Amusement park is $50, plus $10 per person. **What** equation relates the price to the number of people in the group?

Wild World AMUSEMENT PARK

Regular Admission
$21.00 per person

Includes 100-point
BONUS CARD

Special Group Price
$50.00 plus $10.00 per group member

Some things never seem to change. The sun always rises in the east and sets in the west. The United States holds a presidential election every four years. Labor Day always falls on the first Monday of September.

Many other things are always changing. Temperatures rise and fall within a day and from season to season. Store sales change in response to rising and falling prices and shopper demand. Audiences for television shows and movies change as viewers' interests change. The speeds of bikes on streets and roads change in response to variations in traffic, terrain, and weather.

In mathematics, science, and business, quantities that change are called *variables*. Many problems require predicting how changes in the values of one variable are related to changes in the values of another. To help you solve such problems, you can represent the relationships between variables using word descriptions, tables, graphs, and equations. The mathematical ideas and skills used to solve such problems come from the branch of mathematics called *algebra*. This Unit introduces some of the basic tools of algebra.

Mathematical Highlights

Variables and Patterns

I n *Variables and Patterns,* you will study some basic ideas of algebra and learn some ways to use those ideas to solve problems and make decisions.

The Investigations in this Unit will help you learn how to

- Recognize situations in which variables are related in predictable ways

- Describe patterns of change in words, data tables, graphs, and equations

- Use data tables, graphs, equations, and inequalities to solve problems

As you work on the problems in this Unit, ask yourself questions about problem situations that involve related quantitative variables:

What are the variables in the problem?

Which variables depend on or change in relation to others?

How can I use a table, graph, equation, or inequality to represent and analyze a relationship between variables?

Mathematical Practices and Habits of Mind

In the *Connected Mathematics* curriculum you will develop an understanding of important mathematical ideas by solving problems and reflecting on the mathematics involved. Every day, you will use "habits of mind" to make sense of problems and apply what you learn to new situations. Some of these habits are described by the *Common Core State Standards for Mathematical Practices* (MP).

MP1 Make sense of problems and persevere in solving them.

When using mathematics to solve a problem, it helps to think carefully about

- data and other facts you are given and what additional information you need to solve the problem;
- strategies you have used to solve similar problems and whether you could solve a related simpler problem first;
- how you could express the problem with equations, diagrams, or graphs;
- whether your answer makes sense.

MP2 Reason abstractly and quantitatively.

When you are asked to solve a problem, it often helps to

- focus first on the key mathematical ideas;
- check that your answer makes sense in the problem setting;
- use what you know about the problem setting to guide your mathematical reasoning.

MP3 Construct viable arguments and critique the reasoning of others.

When you are asked to explain why a conjecture is correct, you can

- show some examples that fit the claim and explain why they fit;
- show how a new result follows logically from known facts and principles.

When you believe a mathematical claim is incorrect, you can

- show one or more counterexamples—cases that don't fit the claim;
- find steps in the argument that do not follow logically from prior claims.

MP4 Model with mathematics.

When you are asked to solve problems, it often helps to

- think carefully about the numbers or geometric shapes that are the most important factors in the problem, then ask yourself how those factors are related to each other;
- express data and relationships in the problem with tables, graphs, diagrams, or equations, and check your result to see if it makes sense.

MP5 Use appropriate tools strategically.

When working on mathematical questions, you should always

- decide which tools are most helpful for solving the problem and why;
- try a different tool when you get stuck.

MP6 Attend to precision.

In every mathematical exploration or problem-solving task, it is important to

- think carefully about the required accuracy of results; is a number estimate or geometric sketch good enough, or is a precise value or drawing needed?
- report your discoveries with clear and correct mathematical language that can be understood by those to whom you are speaking or writing.

MP7 Look for and make use of structure.

In mathematical explorations and problem solving, it is often helpful to

- look for patterns that show how data points, numbers, or geometric shapes are related to each other;
- use patterns to make predictions.

MP8 Look for and express regularity in repeated reasoning.

When results of a repeated calculation show a pattern, it helps to

- express that pattern as a general rule that can be used in similar cases;
- look for shortcuts that will make the calculation simpler in other cases.

You will use all of the Mathematical Practices in this Unit. Sometimes, when you look at a Problem, it is obvious which practice is most helpful. At other times, you will decide on a practice to use during class explorations and discussions. After completing each Problem, ask yourself:

- What mathematics have I learned by solving this Problem?
- What Mathematical Practices were helpful in learning this mathematics?

Variables, Tables, and Graphs

The bicycle was invented in 1791. Today, people around the world use bicycles for daily transportation and recreation. Many spend their vacations taking organized bicycle tours.

For example, the RAGBRAI, which stands for Register's Annual Great Bicycle Ride Across Iowa, is a weeklong cycling tour across the state of Iowa. Cyclists start by dipping their back bicycle wheels into the Missouri River along Iowa's western border. They end by dipping their front wheels into the Mississippi River on Iowa's eastern border.

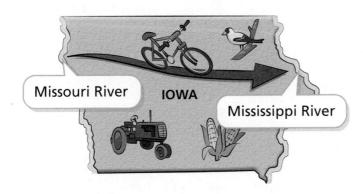

Common Core State Standards

6.RP.A.3a Make tables of equivalent ratios relating quantities with whole-number measurements, find missing values in the tables, and plot the pairs of values on the coordinate plane. Use tables to compare ratios.

6.RP.A.3b Solve unit rate problems including those involving unit pricing and constant speed.

6.EE.C.9 Use variables to represent two quantities in a real-world problem that change in relationship to one another; write an equation to express one quantity, thought of as the dependent variable, in terms of the other quantity, thought of as the independent variable. Analyze the relationship between the dependent and independent variables using graphs and tables, and relate these to the equation.

Also 6.NS.C.6c, 6.NS.C.8

Sidney, Celia, Liz, Malcolm, and Theo heard about the RAGBRAI. The five college students decide to operate bicycle tours as a summer business. They choose a route along the ocean from Atlantic City, New Jersey, to Colonial Williamsburg, Virginia. The students name their new business Ocean Bike Tours.

1.1 Getting Ready to Ride
Data Tables and Graphs

The Ocean Bike Tours business partners think their customers could ride between 60 and 90 miles in a day. Using that guideline, a map, and campground information, they plan a three-day tour route. The business partners also plan for rest stops and visits to interesting places. To finalize plans, they need to answer one more question:

- How are the cyclists' speed and distance likely to change throughout a day?

An answer to that question could only come from a test ride. Because this is difficult to do in school, you can get some ideas by doing a jumping jack experiment. This experiment will test your own physical fitness.

In this experiment, there are two quantities involved, the number of jumping jacks and time. The number of jumping jacks changes over time.

Suppose you did jumping jacks as fast as possible for a 2-minute test period.

- How many jumping jacks do you think you could complete in 2 minutes?

- How do you think your jumping jack rate would change over the 2-minute test?

Problem 1.1

A Do the jumping jack fitness test with help from a timer, a counter, and a recorder. Enter the total number of jumping jacks after every 10 seconds in a data table:

Jumping Jack Experiment

Time (seconds)	0	10	20	30	40	50	60	70	...
Total Number of Jumping Jacks									

B Record your data on a copy of the coordinate grid shown below.

Jumping Jacks Over Time

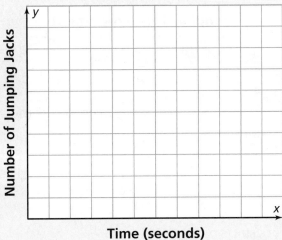

Number of Jumping Jacks

Time (seconds)

continued on the next page >

Problem 1.1 continued

C How did the jumping jack rate (number per second) change over time?

   1. How is the change over time shown in the data table?

   2. How is the change over time shown in the graph?

D Use your jumping jack data. What can you say about the cyclists' speed during the Ocean Bike Tours ride?

E One group said, "Our jumper did 8 jumping jacks for every 10 seconds."

  1. a. Copy and complete the table to show results if a student jumped at a steady pace matching that ratio over 60 seconds.

Jumping Jack Experiment

Time (seconds)	0	10	15	20	▦	30	▦	40	▦	50	▦	60
Total Number of Jumping Jacks	▦	8	12	▦	20	▦	28	▦	36	▦	44	▦

    b. Plot the points corresponding to the (*time, jumping jack total*) pairs in the table on a coordinate grid. Describe the pattern you see.

  2. a. Another group's jumper did 4 jumping jacks for every 6 seconds. Copy and complete the table to show results if a student jumped at a steady pace matching that ratio over 30 seconds.

Jumping Jack Experiment

Time (seconds)	0	6	9	12	▦	▦	30
Total Number of Jumping Jacks	▦	4	▦	▦	10	12	▦

    b. Plot the points corresponding to the (*time, jumping jack total*) pairs in the table on a coordinate grid. Describe the pattern you see. Compare the table and graph patterns in parts (1) and (2).

ACE Homework starts on page 20.

1.2 From Atlantic City to Lewes
Time, Rate, and Distance

In the jumping jack experiment, the number of jumping jacks and time are variables. A **variable** is a quantity that may take on different values. One way in which values of real-life variables may change is with the passage of time. You saw this in the jumping jack experiment. The number of jumping jacks changes based on the elapsed time.

The jumping jack experiment gives some ideas about what cyclists might expect on a daylong trip. To be more confident, the Ocean Bike Tours business partners decide to test their bike tour route.

The cyclists begin their bike tour in Atlantic City, New Jersey, and ride south to Cape May.

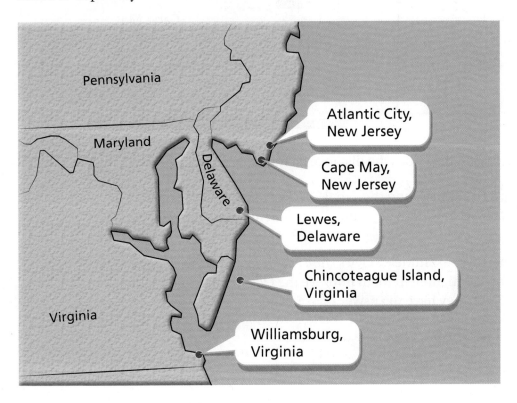

Sidney follows the cyclists in a van with a trailer for camping gear and bicycles. Every half-hour, he records in a table the distances the cyclists have traveled from Atlantic City.

Atlantic City to Cape May	
Time (h)	Distance (mi)
0	0
0.5	8
1.0	15
1.5	19
2.0	25
2.5	27
3.0	34
3.5	31
4.0	38
4.5	40
5.0	45

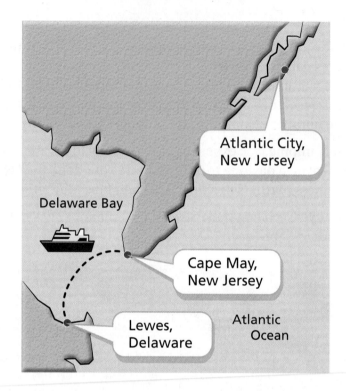

- As time increases, how does the distance change?

From Cape May, the cyclists and the van take a ferry across Delaware Bay to Lewes (LOO-is), Delaware. They camp that night in a state park along the ocean.

The business partners examine Sidney's (*time, distance*) data. They hope to find patterns that might help them improve the Ocean Bike Tours route and schedule. First, they have to answer this question:

- What story does the pattern in the table tell?

Problem 1.2

Ⓐ **1.** Plot the (*time, distance*) data pairs on a coordinate grid.

2. What interesting patterns do you see in the (*time, distance*) data?

3. Explain how the patterns are shown in the table.

4. Explain how the patterns are shown on the graph.

Ⓑ **1.** At what times in the trip were the cyclists traveling fastest? At what times were they traveling slowest?

2. Explain how your answer is shown in the table.

3. Explain how your answer is shown by the pattern of points on the graph.

Ⓒ Connecting the points on a graph can help you see patterns more clearly. It also helps you consider what is happening in the intervals between the points. Different ways of connecting the given data points tell different stories about what happens between the points.

Consider the data (4.5, 40) and (5.0, 45) from the first day of the Ocean Bike Tours trip. Here are five different ways to connect the graph points on the plot of (*time, distance*).

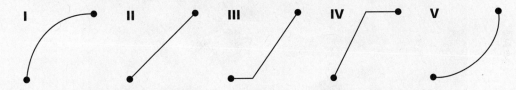

Match the given connecting paths to these travel stories.

1. Celia rode slowly at first and gradually increased her speed.

2. Theo rode quickly and reached the Cape May ferry dock early.

3. Malcolm had to fix a flat tire, so he started after the others.

4. Tony and Sarah started off fast. They soon felt tired and slowed down.

5. Liz pedaled at a steady pace throughout this part of the trip.

Ⓓ What are the advantages and disadvantages of tables or graphs to represent a pattern of change?

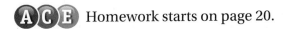 Homework starts on page 20.

1.3 From Lewes to Chincoteague Island
Stories, Tables, and Graphs

On the second day of the bike tour test run, the team leaves Lewes, Delaware, and rides through Ocean City, Maryland. The team stops on Chincoteague (SHING kuh teeg) Island, Virginia. Chincoteague Island is famous for its annual pony auction. Here, the team camps for the night.

Did You Know?

Assateague (A suh teeg) Island is home to herds of wild ponies. The island has a harsh environment of ocean beaches, sand dunes, and marshes. To survive, these sturdy ponies eat salt marsh grasses, seaweed, and even poison ivy.

To keep the population of ponies under control, an auction is held every summer. During the famous "Pony Swim," the ponies for sale swim across a quarter mile of water to Chincoteague Island.

Problem 1.3

Malcolm and Liz drove the tour van on the way from Lewes to Chincoteague. They forgot to record time and distance data. Fortunately, they wrote some notes about the trip.

TripJournal	**All Entries**	June 7

Entry 1: We started at 8:00 A.M. and rode against a strong wind until our midmorning break.

Entry 2: About midmorning, the wind shifted to our backs.

Entry 3: Around noon, we stopped for BBQ lunch and rested for about an hour. By this time we had traveled about halfway to Chinoteague.

Entry 4: Around 2:00 P.M., we stopped for a brief swim in the ocean.

Entry 5: At about 4:00 P.M., all of the riders were tired. There were no bike lanes. So we packed the bikes in the trailer and rode in the van to our campsite in Chincoteague. We took 9 hours to complete today's 80-mile trip.

Edit

A Make a table of (*time, distance*) values to match the story told in Malcolm and Liz's notes.

B Sketch a coordinate graph that shows the information in the table. Does it make sense to connect the points on the graph? Explain your reasoning.

C Explain how the entries in your table and graph illustrate the trip notes.

D Which representation of the data (*table, graph,* or *written notes*) best shows the pattern of change in distance over time? Explain.

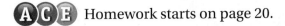

A C E Homework starts on page 20.

1.4 From Chincoteague to Colonial Williamsburg

Average Speed

Malcolm noticed that, on Day 1, the cyclists sometimes went very fast or very slow in any given hour. He also noticed that the cyclists covered 45 miles in 5 hours.

Atlantic City to Cape May

Time (h)	0	0.5	1.0	1.5	2.0	2.5	3.0	3.5	4.0	4.5	5.0
Distance (mi)	0	8	15	19	25	27	34	31	38	40	45

- Malcolm claims that, on average, the cyclists covered 9 miles per hour. Is he correct?

- Did the cyclists actually cover 9 miles per hour in any one hour on Day 1? Explain.

The **average speed** per day is the rate in miles per hour for that day. Malcolm was curious to know what the average speed for Day 3 would be.

On the third day of the bike tour test run, the team travels from its campsite on Chincoteague Island to Williamsburg, Virginia. Here, they visit the restored colonial capital city.

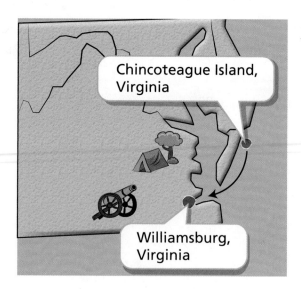

Chincoteague Island, Virginia

Williamsburg, Virginia

Did You Know?

Williamsburg was the political, cultural, and educational center of Virginia from 1699 to 1780. Virginia was the largest, most populous, and most influential of the American colonies.

Near the end of the Revolutionary War, the capital of Virginia was moved to Richmond. For nearly 150 years afterward, Williamsburg was a quiet town.

Then, in 1926, a movement began to restore and preserve the city's historic buildings. Today, Williamsburg is a very popular tourist destination.

Malcolm drove and Sarah rode in the tour van on the way from Chincoteague to Williamsburg. They made a graph showing the cyclists' progress each hour.

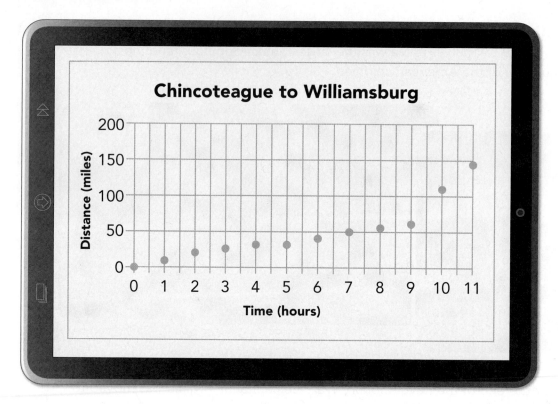

- Describe some interesting patterns that you see in the graph.

Problem 1.4

Ⓐ Make a table of the (*time, distance*) value pairs shown in the graph.

1. What does the point with coordinates (3, 25) tell about the cyclists' progress?

2. Which points on the graph have coordinates (9, 60) and (10, 110)? What do those coordinates tell about the cyclists' time, distance, and speed on Day 3?

3. What was the cyclists' average speed in miles per hour for the trip? How can you find this from the graph? From the table?

Ⓑ The team has to cross the Chesapeake Bay Bridge and Tunnel. Then, they travel on an interstate highway from Norfolk to Williamsburg. So, the team bikes for only the first part of the trip.

1. Based on the graph and your table, when did the team put its bikes on the trailer and begin riding in the van?

2. What was the team's average speed for trip time completed on bikes?

3. What was the team's average speed for trip time completed in the van?

4. How are differences in travel speed shown in the graph?

Ⓒ A very strong cyclist makes the trip from Chincoteague to Williamsburg in 8 hours pedaling at a constant speed.

1. At what speed did the cyclist travel?

2. Describe the graph of (*time, distance*) data for the trip.

ⒶⒸⒺ Homework starts on page 20.

Applications

1. A convenience store has been keeping track of its popcorn sales. The table below shows the total number of bags sold beginning at 6:00 A.M. on a particular day.

Popcorn Sales

Time	Total Bags Sold
6:00 A.M.	0
7:00 A.M.	3
8:00 A.M.	15
9:00 A.M.	20
10:00 A.M.	26
11:00 A.M.	30
noon	45
1:00 P.M.	58
2:00 P.M.	58
3:00 P.M.	62
4:00 P.M.	74
5:00 P.M.	83
6:00 P.M.	88
7:00 P.M.	92

a. Make a coordinate graph of these data. Explain your choice of labels and scales on each axis.

b. Describe the pattern of change in the number of bags of popcorn sold during the day.

c. During which hour did the store sell the most popcorn? During which hour did it sell the least popcorn?

2. When Ming and Jamil studied growth in the population of their city, they found these data:

Population of Okemos

Year	1970	1980	1990	1995	2000	2005	2010
Population (1000's)	20	25	30	35	40	45	50

a. Ming made the graph below.

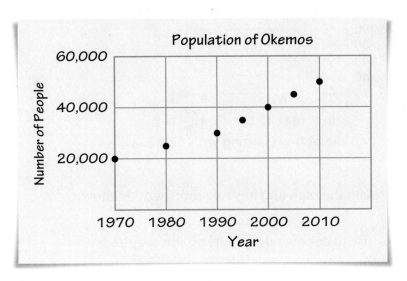

She said, "The graph shows population growing faster in the period from 1995 to 2010 than earlier." Is Ming's claim accurate? Why or why not?

b. Jamil made a different graph. It is shown below.

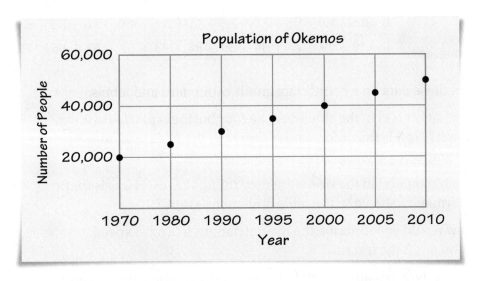

Jamil said, "The graph shows population growing at a steady rate." Is his claim accurate? Why or why not?

3. The graph below shows the numbers of cans of juice purchased each hour from a school's vending machines in one day. On the *x*-axis of the graph, 7 means the time from 7:00 to 8:00, and so on.

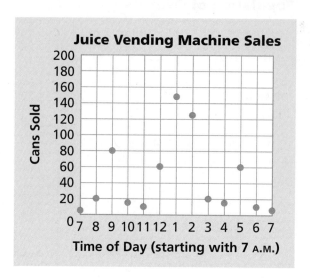

Juice Vending Machine Sales

a. What might explain the high and low sale time periods shown by the graph?

b. Does it make sense to connect the points on this graph? Why or why not?

4. Before deciding that bike tour customers could ride 60–90 miles each day, the Ocean Bike Tours partners went on a test ride. The (*time, distance*) data for their ride are shown in the table below.

Ocean Bike Tours Test Ride

Time (h)	0	0.5	1.0	1.5	2.0	2.5	3.0	3.5	4.0	5.0	5.5	6.0
Distance (mi)	0	10	19	27	34	39	36	43	53	62	66	72

a. Plot these data on a coordinate graph with scales and labels.

b. At what time(s) in the ride were the four business partners riding fastest? How is that information shown in the table and on the graph?

c. At what time(s) in the ride were they riding slowest? How is that information shown in the table and on the graph?

d. How would you describe the overall pattern in cyclist speed throughout the test run?

e. What might explain the dip in the distance data between 2.5 and 3.5 hours?

5. Students have a test to see how many sit-ups they can complete in 10 minutes. Andrea and Ken plot their results. Their graphs are shown below.

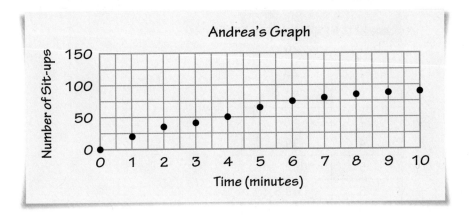

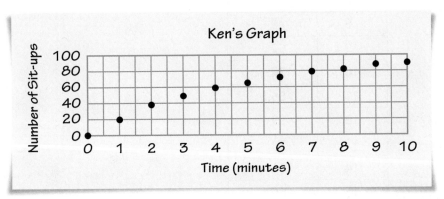

a. Ken claims that he did better because the points on his graph are higher than the points on Andrea's graph. Is Ken correct? Explain.

b. In what ways do the results of the sit-up test show a pattern of endurance in physical activity that is similar to the results of the test ride by the Ocean Bike Tours partners?

c. Which person had the greatest average number of sit-ups per minute?

d. Compare Ken's pace in the first two minutes to his pace in the last two minutes.

6. Katrina's parents kept a record of her growth in height from birth until her 18th birthday. Their data is shown in the table below.

Katrina's Height

Age (yr)	Height (in.)
birth	20
1	29
2	33.5
3	37
4	39.5
5	42
6	45.5
7	47
8	49
9	52
10	54
11	56.5
12	59
13	61
14	64
15	64
16	64
17	64.5
18	64.5

a. Make a coordinate graph of Katrina's height data.

b. During which time interval(s) did Katrina have her greatest "growth spurt"?

c. During which time interval(s) did Katrina's height change the least?

d. Would it make sense to connect the points on the graph? Why or why not?

e. Is it easier to use the table or the graph to answer parts (b) and (c)? Explain.

7. Below is a chart of the water depth in a harbor during a typical 24-hour day. The water level rises and falls with the tides.

Effect of the Tide on Water Depth

Hours Since Midnight	0	1	2	3	4	5	6	7	8
Depth (m)	10.1	10.6	11.5	13.2	14.5	15.5	16.2	15.4	14.6

Hours Since Midnight	9	10	11	12	13	14	15	16
Depth (m)	12.9	11.4	10.3	10.0	10.4	11.4	13.1	14.5

Hours Since Midnight	17	18	19	20	21	22	23	24
Depth (m)	15.4	16.0	15.6	14.3	13.0	11.6	10.7	10.2

a. At what time is the water the deepest? Find the depth at that time.

b. At what time is the water the shallowest? Find the depth at that time.

c. During what time interval does the depth change most rapidly?

d. Make a coordinate graph of the data. Describe the overall pattern you see.

e. How did you choose scales for the *x*-axis and *y*-axis of your graph? Do you think everyone in your class used the same scales? Explain.

8. Three students made graphs of the population of a town called
Huntsville. The break in the *y*-axis in Graphs A and C indicates that
there are values missing between 0 and 8.

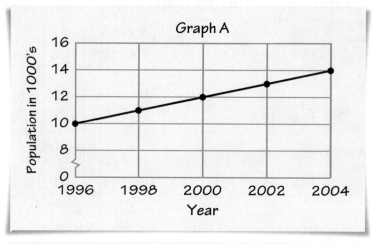

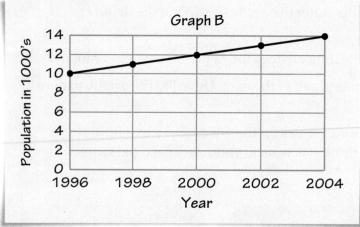

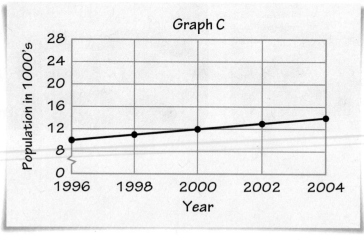

a. Describe the relationship between time and population as shown
in each of the graphs.

b. Is it possible that all three graphs correctly represent the
population growth in Huntsville? Explain.

9. Here is a graph of temperature data collected on the Ocean Bike
Tours test trip from Atlantic City to Lewes.

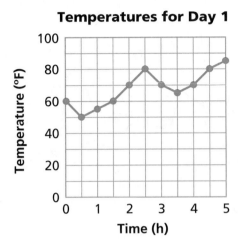

Temperatures for Day 1

a. Make a table of (*time, temperature*) data from this graph.

b. What is the difference between the day's lowest and
highest temperatures?

c. During which time interval(s) did the temperature rise the
fastest? During which time interval did it fall the fastest?

d. Do you prefer using the table or the graph to answer questions
like those in parts (b) and (c)? Explain your reasoning.

e. What information is shown by the lines connecting
the points?

10. Make a table and a graph of (*time, temperature*) data that fit the
following information about a day on the road with the Ocean Bike
Tours cyclists:

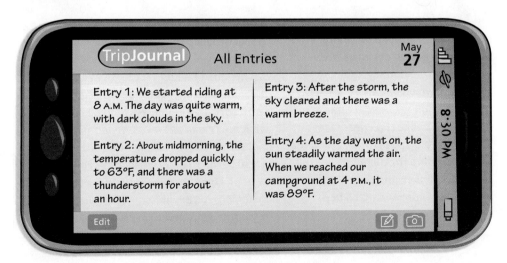

TripJournal   All Entries   May 27

Entry 1: We started riding at 8 A.M. The day was quite warm, with dark clouds in the sky.

Entry 2: About midmorning, the temperature dropped quickly to 63°F, and there was a thunderstorm for about an hour.

Entry 3: After the storm, the sky cleared and there was a warm breeze.

Entry 4: As the day went on, the sun steadily warmed the air. When we reached our campground at 4 P.M., it was 89°F.

8:30 PM

11. Amanda made the graphs below to show how her level of hunger and her happiness changed over the course of a day. She forgot to label the graphs.

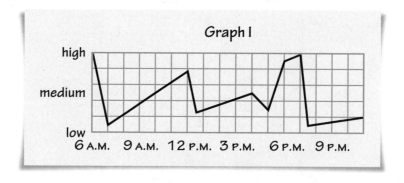

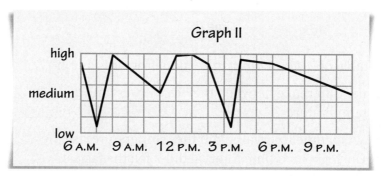

Use the following descriptions to determine which graph shows Amanda's hunger pattern and which graph shows Amanda's happiness. Explain.

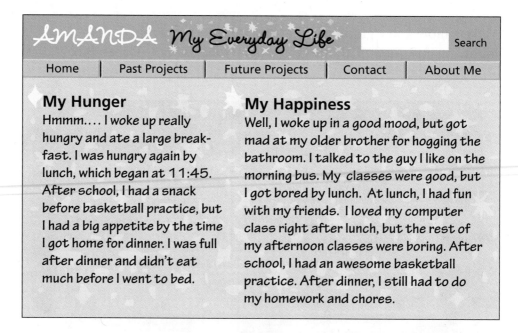

AMANDA *My Everyday Life*   Search

| Home | Past Projects | Future Projects | Contact | About Me |

My Hunger
Hmmm.... I woke up really hungry and ate a large breakfast. I was hungry again by lunch, which began at 11:45. After school, I had a snack before basketball practice, but I had a big appetite by the time I got home for dinner. I was full after dinner and didn't eat much before I went to bed.

My Happiness
Well, I woke up in a good mood, but got mad at my older brother for hogging the bathroom. I talked to the guy I like on the morning bus. My classes were good, but I got bored by lunch. At lunch, I had fun with my friends. I loved my computer class right after lunch, but the rest of my afternoon classes were boring. After school, I had an awesome basketball practice. After dinner, I still had to do my homework and chores.

12. Celia uses (*time, distance*) data from one part of the bike tour test run to draw the following graph relating time and speed. Celia forgot to include scales on the axes of the graph.

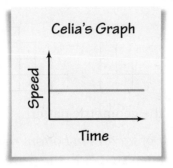

Celia's Graph

a. What does this graph show?

b. Is the graph most likely a picture of speed for a cyclist, the tour van, or the wind over a part of one day's trip? Explain your reasoning about each possibility.

13. The following table shows (*time, distance*) data from the bike tour group's van ride home from Williamsburg to Atlantic City.

Williamsburg to Atlantic City Van Ride

Time (h)	0	1	2	3	4	5	6	7	8
Distance (mi)	0	50	110	150	200	220	280	315	345

a. What was their average speed for the whole trip?

b. What was their average speed for the first four hours of the trip?

c. What was their average speed for the second four hours of the trip?

d. Suppose that for the first four hours of the trip the van had traveled at a steady rate equal to the average speed calculated in part (b). For the second four hours of the trip, suppose the van traveled at a steady rate equal to the average speed calculated in part (c).

   1. Sketch the (*time, distance*) graph that would result from this pattern of driving.

   2. Sketch the (*time, speed*) graph that would result from this pattern of driving.

Connections

14. Consider the pattern below.

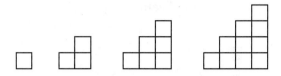

    a. Draw the next shape in the geometric pattern.

    b. Make a table of (*number of squares in bottom row, total number of squares*) data for the first ten shapes in the pattern.

    c. Describe the pattern of increase in total number of squares as length of the bottom row increases.

15. Make a table to show how the total number of cubes in these pyramids changes as the width of the base changes from 3 to 5 to 7. Then use the pattern in those numbers to predict the number of cubes for pyramids with base width of 9, 11, 13, and 15.

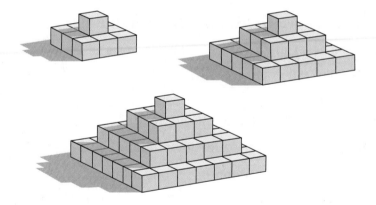

For Exercises 16–18, order the given numbers from least to greatest. Then, for each ordered list, describe a pattern relating each number to the next number.

16. 1.75, 0.25, 0.5, 1.5, 2.0, 0.75, 1.25, 1.00

17. $\frac{3}{8}$, 1, $\frac{1}{4}$, $\frac{7}{8}$, $\frac{3}{4}$, $\frac{1}{2}$, $\frac{1}{8}$, $\frac{5}{8}$

18. $\frac{4}{3}$, $\frac{1}{3}$, $\frac{1}{6}$, $\frac{4}{6}$, $\frac{8}{3}$, $\frac{32}{6}$

19. The partners in Ocean Bike Tours want to compare their plans with other bicycle tour companies. The bike tour they are planning takes three days, and they wonder if this might be too short. Malcolm called 18 different companies and asked, "How many days is your most popular bike trip?" Here are the answers he received:

Bike Tour Data

3	6	7
5	10	7
4	2	3
3	5	14
5	7	12
4	3	6

a. Make a line plot of the data.

b. Based on part (a), should Ocean Bike Tours change the length of the three-day trip? Explain.

20. The graph below shows the results of a survey of people over age 25 who had completed different levels of education. The graph shows the average salary for people with each level of education.

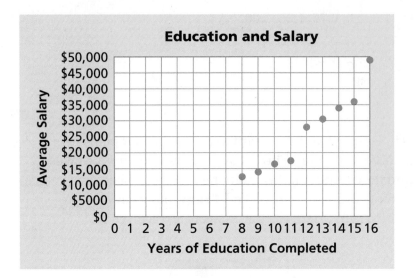

a. Make a table that shows the information in the graph.

b. After how many years of education do salaries take a big jump? Why do you think this happens?

c. Do you find it easier to answer part (b) by looking at the graph or at your table? Explain.

21. Think of something in your life that varies with time. Make a graph to show the pattern of change.

Extensions

22. The number of hours of daylight in a day changes throughout the year. We say that the days are "shorter" in winter and "longer" in summer. The table shows the number of daylight hours in Chicago, Illinois, on a typical day during each month of the year (January is Month 1, and so on).

Daylight Hours

Month	Number of Hours
1	10.0
2	10.2
3	11.7
4	13.1
5	14.3
6	15.0
7	14.5
8	13.8
9	12.5
10	11.0
11	10.5
12	10.0

a. Describe any relationships you see between the two variables.

b. On a grid, sketch a coordinate graph of the data. Put months on the *x*-axis and daylight hours on the *y*-axis. What patterns do you see?

c. The seasons in the Southern Hemisphere are the opposite of the seasons in the Northern Hemisphere. When it is summer in North America, it is winter in Australia. Chicago is about the same distance north of the equator as Melbourne, Australia, is south of the equator. Sketch a graph showing the relationship you would expect to find between the month and the hours of daylight in Melbourne.

d. Put the (*month, daylight*) values from your graph in part (c) into a table.

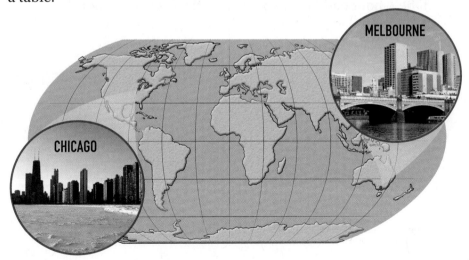

23. a. A school club sells sweatshirts to raise money. Which, if any, of the graphs below describes the relationship you would expect between the price charged for each sweatshirt and the profit? Explain your choice, or draw a new graph that you think better describes this relationship.

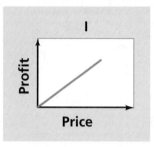

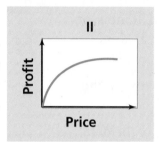

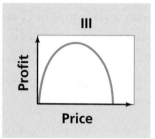

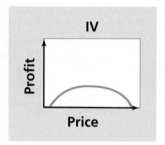

b. What variables might affect the club's profits?

24. Chelsea and Nicole can paddle a canoe at a steady rate of 5 miles per hour in calm water.

a. On Saturday, they paddle for 3 hours on a calm lake. Sketch a graph of their speed over the 3-hour period.

b. On Sunday, they go canoeing on a river with a 2-mile-per-hour current. They paddle with the current for 1 hour. Then, they turn around and paddle against the current for 2 hours. Sketch a graph of their speed over this 3-hour period.

c. When the 3-hour paddle indicated in part (b) was over, how far were Chelsea and Nicole from their starting point?

25. In parts (a)–(e) below, how does the value of one variable change as the value of the other changes? Estimate pairs of values that show the pattern of change you would expect. Record your estimates in a table with at least five data points.

Sample: hours of television you watch in a week and your school grade-point average

Answer: As television time increases, I expect my grade-point average to decrease. See the table below.

TV Time (hours per week)	0	5	10	15	20
Grade Point Average	3.5	3.25	3.0	2.75	2.5

a. distance from school to your home and time it takes to walk home

b. price of popcorn at a theater and number of bags sold

c. speed of an airplane and time it takes the plane to complete a 500-mile trip

d. monthly cell phone bill and number of text messages sent

e. cost of a long-distance telephone call and length of the call in minutes

26. Some students did a jumping jack experiment. They reported data on the student who could do the most jumping jacks in a certain amount of time.

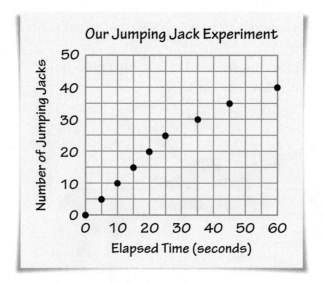

Our Jumping Jack Experiment

a. According to the graph, how many jumping jacks did the jumper make by the end of 10 seconds? By the end of 20 seconds? By the end of 60 seconds?

b. Give the elapsed time and number of jumping jacks for two other points on the graph.

c. What estimate would make sense for the number of jumping jacks in 30 seconds? The number in 40 seconds? The number in 50 seconds?

d. What does the overall pattern in the graph show about the rate at which the test jumper completed jumping jacks?

e. Suppose you connected the first and last data points with a straight line. Would this line show the overall pattern? Explain.

The Problems in this Investigation helped you to think about variables and patterns relating values of variables. In particular, they helped you develop understanding and skill in the use of data tables and graphs in order to study quantities or variables that change over time.

This Investigation challenged you to use those mathematical tools to find important patterns in the relationships between distance, time, and speed of moving objects.

Think about these questions. Discuss your ideas with other students and your teacher. Then write a summary of your findings in your notebook.

1. You can show patterns of change over time with tables, graphs, and written reports.

   a. **What** are the advantages and disadvantages of showing patterns with tables?

   b. **What** are the advantages and disadvantages of showing patterns with graphs?

   c. **What** are the advantages and disadvantages of showing patterns with written reports?

2. a. **How** do you see patterns in the speed of a moving object by studying (*time*, *distance*) data in tables?

   b. **How** do you see patterns in the speed of a moving object by studying (*time*, *distance*) data in coordinate graphs?

Common Core Mathematical Practices

As you worked on the Problems in this Investigation, you used prior knowledge to make sense of them. You also applied Mathematical Practices to solve the Problems. Think back over your work, the ways you thought about the Problems, and how you used Mathematical Practices.

Hector described his thoughts in the following way:

Our group made a table and a graph of our jumping jack experiment. We evaluated the data.

We noticed something about two adjacent table entries. The difference between those entries, divided by 10, tells the number of jumping jacks per second.

However, on our graph, greater rates are shown by bigger jumps upward from one data point to the next.

Common Core Standards for Mathematical Practice
MP4 Model with mathematics.

 • What other Mathematical Practices can you identify in Hector's reasoning?

• Describe a Mathematical Practice that you and your classmates used to solve a different Problem in this Investigation.

Investigation 2

Analyzing Relationships Among Variables

The test run by the Ocean Bike Tours partners raised many questions.

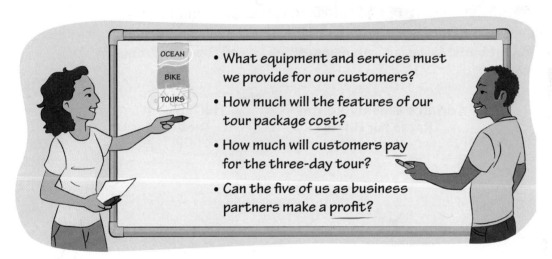

OCEAN BIKE TOURS

- What equipment and services must we provide for our customers?
- How much will the features of our tour package cost?
- How much will customers pay for the three-day tour?
- Can the five of us as business partners make a profit?

To make their choices, the five partners decided to do some research. In this Investigation you will use tables, graphs, and words to analyze information from their research and advise the tour business partners.

Common Core State Standards

6.NS.C.6b Understand signs of numbers in ordered pairs as indicating locations in quadrants of the coordinate plane; recognize that when two ordered pairs differ only by signs, the locations of the points are related by reflections across one or both axes.

6.NS.C.6c Find and position integers and other rational numbers on a horizontal or vertical number line diagram; find and position pairs of integers and other rational numbers on a coordinate plane.

6.NS.C.8 Solve real-world and mathematical problems by graphing points in all four quadrants of the coordinate plane. Include use of coordinates . . . to find distances between points with the same first coordinate or the same second coordinate.

6.EE.B.6 Use variables to represent numbers and write expressions when solving a real-world or mathematical problem; understand that a variable can represent an unknown number, or, depending on the purpose at hand, any number in a specified set.

Also 6.NS.C.6, 6.EE.C.9

2.1 Renting Bicycles
Independent and Dependent Variables

The tour operators decide to rent bicycles for their customers. They get information from two bike shops. Rocky's Cycle Center sends a table of rental fees for bikes.

Rocky's Cycle Center

Bike Rental at Rocky's

Number of Bikes	5	10	15	20	25	30	35	40	45	50
Rental Cost ($)	400	535	655	770	875	975	1,070	1,140	1,180	1,200

Adrian's Bike Shop sends a graph of their rental prices. The number of bikes rented is called the **independent variable**. The rental cost is called the **dependent variable**, because the rental cost depends on the number of bikes rented.

Adrian's Bike Shop

Graphs usually have the independent variable on the *x*-axis and the dependent variable on the *y*-axis.

The Ocean Bike Tour partners need to choose a bike rental shop. Suppose that they ask for your advice.

- Which shop would you recommend?

- How would you justify your choice?

Problem 2.1

Use entries in the table and the graph to answer the following comparison questions.

A What are the costs of renting from Rocky and Adrian if the tour needs 20 bikes? 40 bikes? 32 bikes?

B About how many bikes can be rented from Rocky or Adrian in the following cases?

    1. A group has $900 to spend.

    2. A group has $400 to spend.

C You want to see how rental cost is related to number of bikes.

    1. What pattern do you see in the table from Rocky's Cycle Center?

    2. What pattern do you see in the graph from Adrian's Bike Shop?

D How can you predict rental costs for numbers of bikes that are not shown by entries in the table or points on the graph?

E What information about bike rental costs was easier to get from the table and what from the graph?

F Which data format is most useful?

A C E Homework starts on page 50.

2.2 Finding Customers
Linear and Nonlinear Patterns

The tour operators have planned a route and chosen a bike rental shop. The next task is to figure out a price to charge for the tour. They want the price low enough to attract customers. They also want it high enough to have **income** that is greater than their expenses. That way their business makes a **profit.**

The partners conduct a survey to help set the price. They ask people who have taken other bicycle tours what they would pay for the planned bike tour.

Prices That Customers Would Pay

Tour Price	$100	$150	$200	$250	$300	$350	$400	$450	$500
Number of Customers	40	35	30	25	20	15	10	5	0

Look carefully at the data relating price and number of customers.

Problem 2.2

The following questions can help you choose a tour price.

A 1. Make a graph of the data relating price and number of customers. Which is the independent variable? Which is the dependent variable? Explain how you know.

2. How does the number of customers change as the price increases?

3. How is the change in number of customers shown in the table? How is the change shown by the graph?

4. How would you estimate the number of customers for a price of $175? For a price of $325?

B 1. The partners need to know what income to expect from the tour. They extend the (*price, customers*) table as shown below. Copy and complete the table to find how income would be related to price and number of customers.

Predicting Tour Income

Tour Price	$100	$150	$200	$250	$300	$350	$400	$450	$500
Number of Customers	40	35	30	25	20	15	10	5	0
Tour Income	$4,000	▪	▪	▪	▪	▪	▪	▪	▪

2. Make a graph of the (*price, income*) data.

3. Describe the pattern relating tour income to tour price. Use a sentence that begins, "As tour price increases, tour income . . . ." Explain why that pattern does or does not make sense.

A C E Homework starts on page 50.

2.3 Predicting Profits
Four-Quadrant Graphing

The survey conducted by Ocean Bike Tours showed that income depends on the tour price. The partners want to see if they can make any profit from their business. As well as income, they have to consider the costs of operating the tour. Their research shows that bike rental, camping fees, and food will cost $150 per customer.

The partners want to make a profit. They need to figure out how profit depends on the tour price.

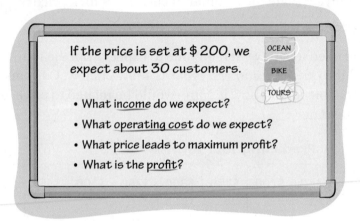

If the price is set at $200, we expect about 30 customers.

OCEAN BIKE TOURS

- What income do we expect?
- What operating cost do we expect?
- What price leads to maximum profit?
- What is the profit?

Problem 2.3

A   **1.** The table below shows the relationship between profit and price. Copy and complete the table.

Predicted Tour Profit

Tour Price	$100	$150	$200	$250	$300	$350	$400	$450	$500
Number of Customers	40	35	30	25	20	15	10	5	0
Tour Income ($)	4,000	■	■	■	■	■	■	■	■
Operating Cost ($)	6,000	■	■	■	■	■	■	■	■
Tour Profit or Loss ($)	−2,000	■	■	■	■	■	■	■	■

Problem **2.3** *continued*

2. Celia and Malcolm want a picture of profit prospects for the tour business. They need to graph the (*price, profit*) data. Some of the data are negative numbers. Those numbers represent possible losses for the tour operation.

   The key to graphing data that are negative numbers is to extend the *x*- and *y*-axis number lines. Both the *x*- and *y*-axes can be extended in the negative direction. This gives a grid like the one shown below. Use the grid to sketch a graph for the (*price, profit*) data points from the table in part (1).

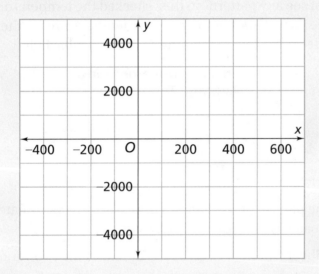

3. **a.** Describe the pattern in the table in part (1) and the graph in part (2).

   b. Explain why the pattern occurs.

   c. Think about the analysis of profit predictions. What tour price would you suggest? Explain your reasoning.

continued on the next page >

Problem 2.3 *continued*

B In January, the partners thought about offering a winter bike tour. They looked at the forecast for the next four days. They wrote down the number of degrees above or below each day's average temperature.

Degrees Above or Below Average Temperature

x	0	1	2	3	4
y	−1	5	−3	−5	2

They did not see any pattern, so they checked the temperatures for the previous five days. They compared those temperatures to the average. They recorded their data for all nine days in the table below.

Degrees Above or Below Average Temperature

x	−4	−3	−2	−1	0	1	2	3	4
y	−2	4	−3	1	−1	5	−3	−5	2

1. What do the *x*- and *y*-values represent?

2. Plot the pairs of (*x*, *y*) values in the table on a coordinate grid. Label each point with its coordinates.

3. Describe the pattern of change that relates the two variables.

C 1. Suppose that you are standing at the point with coordinates (3, 4). Tell how you would move on the grid lines to reach the points below.

    a. (−3, 4)   **b.** (−3, −4)   **c.** (3, −4)

    d. (1.5, −2)   **e.** (−1.5, 2)   **f.** (−2.5, −3.5)

2. How far would you have to move on the grid lines to travel between each pair of points?

    a. (3, 4) to (−3, 4)   **b.** (3, 4) to (3, −4)   **c.** (3, 4) to (−3, −4)

D 1. Jakayla was looking at the points (3, 4), (−3, 4), (−3, −4), and (3, −4). She said that the locations of the points with different signs are mirror images of each other. Does Jakayla's conjecture make sense? Explain.

2. Mitch says this is like a reflection. Does Mitch's comment make sense?

ACE Homework starts on page 50.

2.4 What's the Story?
Interpreting Graphs

Information about variables is often given by coordinate graphs.
So, it is important to be good at reading the "story" in a graph.
Here are some questions to ask when you look at a graph.

- What are the variables?

- Do the values of one variable seem to depend on the values of
  the other?

- What does the shape of the graph say about the relationship
  between the variables?

For example, the number of cars in your school's parking lot changes
as time passes during a typical school day. Graph 1 and Graph 2 show
two possibilities for the way the number of parked cars might change
over time.

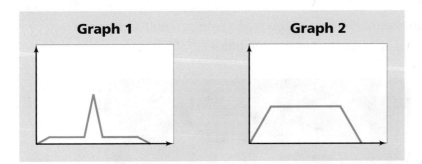

- Describe the story each graph tells about the school parking lot.

- Which graph shows the pattern you expect?

- How could you label the graph you chose so that someone
  else would know what it represents?

Problem 2.4

Questions A–H describe pairs of related variables.
For each pair, do the following.

- Decide what the variables are.
- Decide which variable is the dependent variable and which is the independent variable.
- Think about what a graph or table of these data would look like.
- Find the graph at the end of the Problem that tells the story of how the variables are related. If no graph fits the relationship as you understand it, sketch a graph of your own.
- Explain what the graph tells about the relationship of the variables.
- Give the graph a title.

A The number of students who go on a school trip is related to the price of the trip for each student.

B When a skateboard rider goes down one side of a half-pipe ramp and up the other side, her speed changes as time passes.

C The water level changes over time when someone fills a tub, takes a bath, and empties the tub.

D The waiting time for a popular ride at an amusement park is related to the number of people in the park.

Problem **2.4** *continued*

E The daily profit or loss of an amusement park depends on the number of paying customers.

F The number of hours of daylight changes over time as the seasons change.

G The daily profit or loss of an outdoor skating rink depends on the daytime high temperature.

H Weekly attendance at a popular movie changes as time passes from the date the movie first appears in theaters.

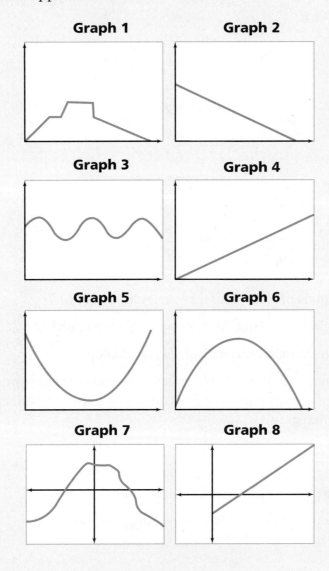

Graph 1 **Graph 2**

Graph 3 **Graph 4**

Graph 5 **Graph 6**

Graph 7 **Graph 8**

A C E Homework starts on page 50.

Applications

1. The following table shows typical weights for young tiger cubs from birth to 11 weeks. Use the data to answer parts (a)–(g).

Typical Weights for Tiger Cubs

Age (weeks)	Expected Body Weight (kg)
birth	1.3
1	2.3
2	3.0
3	3.8
4	4.5
5	5.2
6	6.0
7	6.7
8	7.5
9	7.6
10	8.9
11	9.7

a. What weight is predicted for a 1-week-old tiger cub?

b. What weight is predicted for a 10-week-old tiger cub?

c. At what age do tiger cubs typically weigh 7 kilograms?

d. Plot the (*age, weight*) data on a coordinate grid with appropriate scales. Explain why it does or does not make sense to connect the points on that graph.

e. How would you describe the pattern relating tiger cub age and weight?

f. How is the pattern shown in the data table?

g. How is the pattern shown in the coordinate graph?

2. Desi is planning a go-kart party. Kartland gives him a table of group rates. Thunder Alley gives him a graph. The table and graph are shown below.

Kartland Price Packages

Number of Laps Raced	10	20	30	40	50	60
Cost	$25	$45	$65	$85	$105	$125

a. Find the cost at both locations for 50 laps.

b. Find the cost at both locations for 20 laps.

c. Find the cost at both locations for 35 laps.

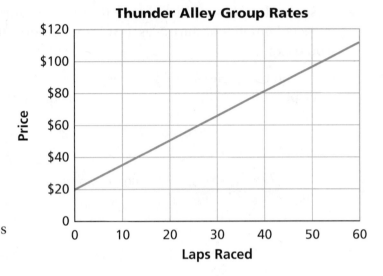

d. Look for patterns in the relationships between number of laps and cost at Thunder Alley. How is the pattern shown in the table?

e. Look for patterns in the relationships between number of laps and cost at Kartland. How is the pattern shown in the graph?

f. Which location seems to offer the better deal?

3. The following table shows the fees charged for campsites at one of the campgrounds on the Ocean Bike Tours route.

Campground Fees

Number of Campsites	1	2	3	4	5	6	7	8
Total Fee	$12.50	$25.00	$37.50	$50.00	$62.50	$75.00	$87.50	$100.00

a. Make a coordinate graph of the data.

b. Does it make sense to connect the points on the graph? Explain.

c. Using the table, describe the pattern of change in the total campground fee as the number of campsites increases.

d. How is the pattern you described in part (c) shown in your graph?

4. Some class officers want to sell T-shirts to raise funds for a class trip. They ask the students in their class how much they would pay for a shirt and recorded the data in a table.

Projected Shirt Sales

Price per Shirt	$5	$10	$15	$20	$25
Number of Shirt Sales	50	40	30	20	10

a. Describe the relationship between the price per shirt and the expected number of shirt sales. Is this the sort of pattern you would expect?

b. Copy and complete this table to show the relationship between price per shirt and the expected total value of the shirt sales.

Projected Shirt Sales

Price per Shirt	$5	$10	$15	$20	$25
Number of Shirt Sales	50	40	30	20	10
Value of Shirt Sales	$250	$400	▦	▦	▦

c. How would you describe the relationship between price per shirt and expected total value of shirt sales? Is this the sort of pattern you would expect?

d. Make coordinate graphs of the data like the ones started below.

e. Explain how your answers to parts (a) and (c) are shown in the graphs.

5. A camping-supply store rents camping gear for $25 per person for a week.

   a. Make a table of the total rental charges for 0, 5, 10, ... , 40 campers.

   b. Make a coordinate graph using the data in your table.

   c. Compare the pattern in your table and graph with patterns you found in the campground fee data in Exercise 3. Describe the similarities and differences between the two sets of data.

6. The bike tour partners need to rent a truck to transport camping gear, clothes, and bicycle repair equipment. They check prices at two truck-rental companies.

   a. East Coast Trucks charges $4 for each mile driven. Make a table of the charges for 0, 100, 200, ... , 800 miles.

   b. Philadelphia Truck Rental charges $40 per day and an additional $3.00 for each mile driven. Make a table of the charges for renting a truck for five days and driving it 0, 100, 200, ... , 800 miles.

   c. On one coordinate graph, plot the charges for both rental companies. Use different colors to mark points representing the two companies' plans.

   d. Based on your work in parts (a)–(c), which company offers the better deal? Explain.

7. The table below shows fees for using a campsite at a state park for 1 day up to the park limit of 10 days.

Campsite Fees

Days of Use	1	2	3	4	5	6	7	8	9	10
Total Fee	$20	$30	$40	$50	$60	$70	$75	$80	$85	$90

   a. Make a coordinate graph representing data in the table.

   b. Does it make sense to connect the points on your graph? Explain.

   c. Describe the pattern relating the variables *days of use* and *campsite fee*.

8. The graph at the right shows the relationship between daily profit and outdoor temperature at an indoor water park on ten days at various times of the year.

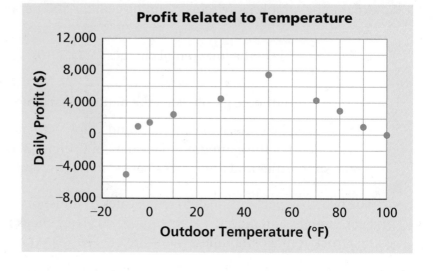

a. Complete a table showing the data values represented.

b. Describe the pattern relating profit to outdoor temperature. Explain how the pattern is shown by the points of the graph.

9. Coordinate graphs with four quadrants can also be used for locating places on a map. The four boxes in the table below show where in the four quadrants the x- and y-values will be positive and negative.

(−, +)	(+, +)
(−, −)	(+, −)

Use the table and the map grid to give coordinates locating each labeled site. Write the coordinates as (x, y).

a. City Hall

b. hospital

c. stadium

d. police station

e. fire station

f. middle school

g. high school

h. shopping mall

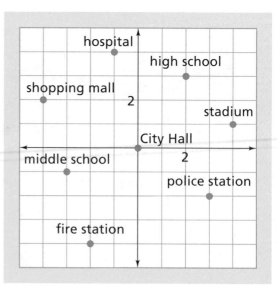

Suppose a motion detector tracks the time and the distance traveled as you walk 40 feet in 8 seconds. The results are shown in the graphs below. Use them to answer Exercises 10–11.

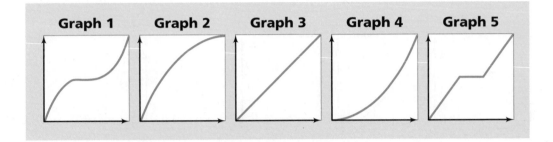

Graph 1   Graph 2   Graph 3   Graph 4   Graph 5

10. Match one of the (*time, distance*) graphs above with the story that describes each walk.

   a. You walk at a steady pace of 5 feet per second.

   b. You walk slowly at first, and then steadily increase your walking speed.

   c. You walk rapidly at first, pause for several seconds, and then walk at an increasing rate for the rest of the trip.

   d. You walk at a steady rate for 3 seconds, pause for 2 seconds, and then walk at a steady rate for the rest of the trip.

   e. You walk rapidly at first, but gradually slow down as you reach the end of the walk.

11. For each walk in the graphs above, complete a (*time, distance*) table like the one begun below. Use numbers that will match the pattern shown in the graph.

Time (seconds)	1	2	3	4	5	6	7	8
Distance (feet)	■	■	■	■	■	■	■	40

12. The graphs below show five patterns for the daily sales of a new video game as time passed after its release. Match each (*time, sales*) graph with the "story" it tells.

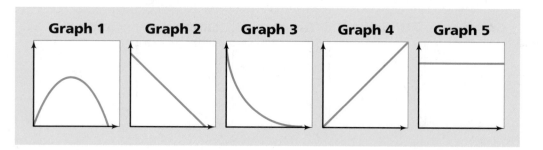

Graph 1 **Graph 2** **Graph 3** **Graph 4** **Graph 5**

a. The daily sales declined at a steady rate.

b. The daily sales did not change.

c. The daily sales rose rapidly, then leveled off, and then declined rapidly.

d. The daily sales rose at a steady rate.

e. The daily sales dropped rapidly at first and then at a slower rate.

13. Multiple Choice Jamie is going to Washington, D.C., to march in a parade with his school band. He plans to set aside $25 at the end of each month to use for the trip. Choose the graph that shows how Jamie's savings will grow as time passes.

A.
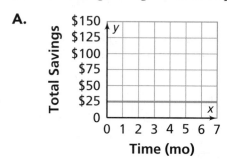

B.
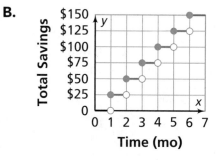

C.
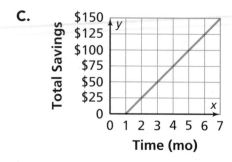

D. None of these is correct.

14. The graph below shows how the temperature changed during an all-day hike by students in the Terrapin Middle School science club.

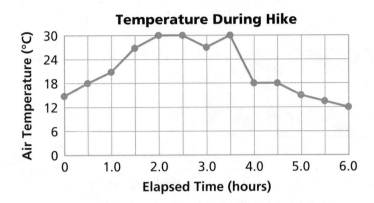

Temperature During Hike

a. What was the maximum temperature and when did it occur?

b. When was the temperature rising most rapidly?

c. When was the temperature falling most rapidly?

d. When was the temperature about 24°C?

e. The hikers encountered a thunderstorm with rain. When do you think this happened?

Jacy works at a department store on the weekends. The graph at the right shows parking costs at the garage Jacy uses.

15. Multiple Choice How much will Jacy spend to park for less than half an hour?

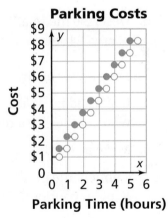

Parking Costs

F. $0.50

G. $0.75

H. $1.00

J. $1.50

16. Multiple Choice How much will Jacy spend to park for 4 hours and 15 minutes?

A. $6.00

B. $6.50

C. $6.75

D. $7.00

Connections

17. The area of a rectangle is the product of its length and its width.

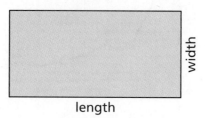

length

width

a. Find all whole-number pairs of length and width values that give an area of 24 square meters. Copy and extend the table here to record the pairs.

Rectangles With Area 24 m²

Length	▪	▪	▪	...
Width	▪	▪	▪	...

b. Make a coordinate graph of the (*length, width*) data from part (a).

c. Connect the points on your graph if it makes sense to do so. Explain your decision.

d. Describe the relationship between length and width for rectangles of area 24 square meters.

18. The perimeter of any rectangle is the sum of its side lengths.

a. Make a table of all possible whole-number pairs of length and width values for a rectangle with a perimeter of 18 meters.

b. Make a coordinate graph of the (*length, width*) data from part (a).

c. Connect the points on your graph if it makes sense to do so. Explain your decision.

d. Describe the relationship between length and width for rectangles of perimeter 18 meters. Explain how that relationship is shown in the table and graph.

19. The table below shows the winning countries and the winning times for the women's Olympic 400-meter dash since 1964.

Women's Olympic 400-meter Dash

Year	Country	Time (seconds)
1964	Australia	52.01
1968	France	52.03
1972	East Germany	51.08
1976	Poland	49.29
1980	East Germany	48.88
1984	United States	48.83
1988	Union of Soviet Socialist Republics	48.65
1992	France	48.83
1996	France	48.25
2000	Australia	49.11
2004	Bahamas	49.41
2008	United Kingdom	49.62
2012	United States	49.55

a. Make a coordinate graph of the (*year, time*) information. Choose a scale that allows you to see the differences between the winning times.

b. What patterns do you see in the table and graph? Do the winning times seem to be rising or falling? In which year was the best time earned?

20. Here are the box-office earnings for a movie during each of the first eight weeks following its release.

Box Office Earnings

Weeks in Theaters	1	2	3	4	5	6	7	8
Weekly Earnings ($ millions)	16	22	18	12	7	4	3	1

  a. Make a coordinate graph showing the data from the table.

  b. Explain how the weekly earnings changed as time passed. How is this pattern of change shown in the table and the graph? Why might this change have occurred?

  c. What were the total earnings of the movie in the eight weeks?

  d. Make a coordinate graph showing the total earnings after each week.

  e. Explain how the movie's total earnings changed over time. How is this pattern of change shown in the table and the graph? Why might this change have occurred?

21. Two students were thinking about the relationship between price and number of T-shirt sales in a school fundraiser. They had different ideas about independent and dependent variables.

> Shaun argued that changing the price would change the number sold, so price is the independent variable.
>
> Victoria argued that the goal for number sold would dictate the price to be charged, so number of sales is the independent variable.

What do you think of these two ideas? Does it always matter which variable is considered independent and which dependent?

Extensions

22. Students plan to hold a car wash to raise money. The students ask some adults how much they would pay for a car wash. The table below shows the results of the research.

Price Customers Would Pay for a Car Wash

Car Wash Price	$4	$6	$8	$10	$12	$14
Number of Customers	120	105	90	75	60	45

a. Make a coordinate graph of the (*price, customers*) data. Connect the points if it makes sense to do so.

b. Describe the pattern relating the price to the number of customers. Explain how the table and the graph show the pattern.

c. Based on the pattern, what number of customers would you predict if the price were $16? If the price were $20? If the price were $2?

d. Copy and complete the following table relating car wash price to projected income.

Projected Car Wash Income

Car Wash Price	$4	$6	$8	$10	$12	$14
Number of Customers	120	105	90	75	60	45
Projected Income	▩	▩	▩	▩	▩	▩

e. Make a coordinate graph of the (*price, income*) data.

f. Explain why it makes sense to consider price the independent variable and income the dependent variable.

g. Does it make sense to connect the points on the coordinate graph data plot? Why or why not?

h. Describe the way projected car wash income changes as the price increases. Explain how this pattern is shown in the graph.

i. Suppose the students must pay $1.50 per car for water and cleaning supplies. How can you use this factor to find the profit from the car wash for various prices?

23. Use what you know about decimals to find coordinates of five points that lie on the line segment between the labeled points on each of these graphs:

a.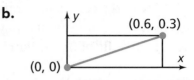

24. Each of the graphs below shows a relationship between independent (*x*-axis) and dependent (*y*-axis) variables. However, the scales on the coordinate axes are not the same for all the graphs.

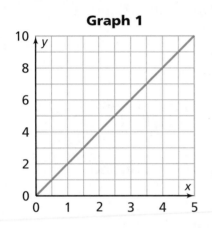

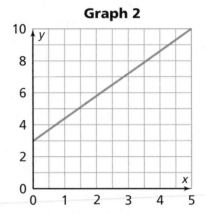

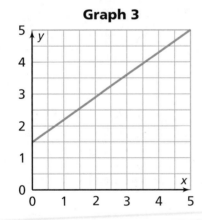

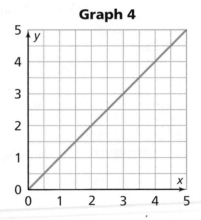

a. For each graph complete this statement: The graph shows that *y* increases by ▆ for every increase of 1 in *x*.

b. Which graph shows the dependent variable increasing most rapidly as the independent variable increases?

c. Which graph shows the dependent variable increasing most slowly as the independent variable increases?

In this Investigation, you looked at patterns relating the values of variables. You also thought about the ways that those patterns are shown in tables of values and coordinate graphs. The following questions will help you to summarize what you have learned.

Think about these questions. Discuss your ideas with other students and your teacher. Then write a summary of your findings in your notebook.

1. The word *variable* is used often to describe conditions in science and business.

   a. **Explain** what the word *variable* means when it is used in situations like those you studied in this Investigation.

   b. **When** are the words *independent* and *dependent* used to describe related variables? How are they used?

2. Suppose the values of a dependent variable increase as the values of a related independent variable increase. **How** is the relationship of the variables shown in each of the following?

   a. a table of values for the two variables

   b. a graph of values for the two variables

3. Suppose the values of a dependent variable decrease as the values of a related independent variable increase. **How** is the relationship of the variables shown in each of the following?

   a. a table of values for the two variables

   b. a graph of values for the two variables

Common Core Mathematical Practices

As you worked on the Problems in this Investigation, you used prior knowledge to make sense of the Problems. You also applied Mathematical Practices to solve the Problems. Think back over your work, the ways you thought about the Problems, and how you used Mathematical Practices.

Jayden described his thoughts in the following way:

> We looked at two bicycle shops in Problem 2.1. We noticed that, for both shops, the rental cost increases as the number of bikes increases.
>
> The cost for renting from Rocky starts higher. Beyond a certain point, Rocky's cost increases more slowly than the cost for renting from Adrian.
>
> Another group noticed that Adrian charges a flat rate of $30 per bike. Rocky's charge per bike decreases as the number of bikes increases.
>
> Then Mike, in a third group, graphed the costs for renting from Rocky. He noticed that the pattern resembles the pattern for jumping jacks. The points rise rapidly at first, but then the rate of increase gets smaller.

Common Core Standards for Mathematical Practice

MP8 Look for and express regularity in repeated reasoning.

- What other Mathematical Practices can you identify in Jayden's reasoning?

- Describe a Mathematical Practice that you and your classmates used to solve a different Problem in this Investigation.

Investigation 3

Relating Variables With Equations

In the first two Investigations of this Unit, you used tables and graphs to study relationships between variables. It is helpful to express those relationships with rules. Those rules tell how to calculate the value of the dependent variable given the value of the independent variable.

In many cases, you can write the rules as algebraic equations or formulas. Working on the Problems of this Investigation will help you develop that skill.

Representations of Relationships
Problem Context

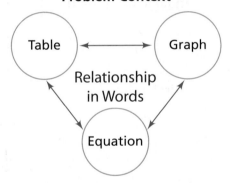

Common Core State Standards

6.EE.A.2 Write, read, and evaluate expressions in which letters stand for numbers.

6.EE.A.2c Evaluate expressions at specific values of their variables. Include expressions that arise from formulas used in real-world problems. Perform arithmetic operations, including those involving whole-number exponents, in the conventional order when there are no parentheses to specify a particular order (Order of Operations).

6.EE.B.7 Solve real-world and mathematical problems by writing and solving equations of the form $x + p = q$ and $px = q$ for cases in which p, q and x are all nonnegative rational numbers.

6.EE.C.9 Use variables to represent two quantities in a real-world problem that change in relationship to one another; write an equation to express one quantity, thought of as the dependent variable, in terms of the other quantity, thought of as the independent variable. Analyze the relationship between the dependent and independent variables using graphs and tables, and relate these to the equation.

Also **6.RP.A.2, 6.RP.A.3, 6.RP.A.3a, 6.RP.A.3b, 6.RP.A.3d, 6.EE.A.1, 6.EE.A.2a, 6.EE.A.3, 6.EE.A.4, 6.EE.B.6**

3.1   Visit to Wild World
Equations With One Operation

On the last day of the Ocean Bike Tours trip, the riders will be near Wild World Amusement Park. They want to plan a stop there.

- What variables would affect the cost of the amusement park trip?

- How would those variables affect the cost?

Malcolm finds out that it costs $21 per person to visit Wild World. Liz suggests that they make a table or graph relating admission price to the number of people. However, Malcolm says there is a simple rule for calculating the cost:

The cost in dollars is equal to 21 times the number of people.

He wrote the rule as the statement:

$$cost = 21 \times number\ of\ people$$

Liz shortens Malcolm's statement by using single letters to stand for the variables. She uses c to stand for the cost and n to stand for the number of people:

$$c = 21 \times n$$

Note on Notation When you multiply a number by a letter variable, you can leave out the multiplication sign. So, $21n$ means $21 \times n$.

You can shorten the statement even more:

$$c = 21n$$

So, $21n$ is an **expression** for the total cost C. You obtain the total cost by multiplying 21, the cost per person, by n, the number of people. The fact that C and $21n$ are equal gives the **equation** $C = 21n$. Here, the number 21 is called the **coefficient** of the variable n.

The equation $c = 21n$ involves one calculation. You multiply the number of customers n by the cost per customer, $21. Many common equations involve one calculation.

Problem 3.1

A Theo wants to attract customers for the bike tour. He suggests a discount of $50 off the regular price for early registration.

1. What is the discounted price if the regular tour price is is $400? $500? $650?

2. Write an equation that represents the relationship of discounted price D to regular tour price P.

OCEAN BIKE TOURS

Home
Trip Dates
Rates
Maps
Safety
Video

PRICE DISCOUNT

$50 *off regular price*

Early Registration!

B When the Ocean Bike Tours partners set a price for customers, they need to find the 6% sales tax.

1. What is the sales tax if the tour price is $400? $500? $650?

2. Write an equation that represents the relationship of the amount of sales tax T to tour price P.

C Suppose a professional cyclist sustained a speed of about 20 miles per hour over a long race.

1. About how far would the cyclist travel in 2 hours? 3 hours? 3.5 hours?

2. At a speed of 20 miles per hour, how is the distance traveled d related to the time t (in hours)? Write an equation to represent the relationship.

3. Explain what information the coefficient of t represents.

D The trip from Williamsburg, Virginia, to Atlantic City, New Jersey, is about 350 miles.

1. How long will the trip take if the average speed of the van is 40 miles per hour? 50 miles per hour? 60 miles per hour?

2. Write an equation that shows how total trip time t depends on average driving speed s.

A C E Homework starts on page 76.

3.2 Moving, Texting, and Measuring
Using Rates and Rate Tables

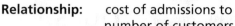

There are many relationships between variables that you can write as algebraic equations. One simple type is especially important.

Relationship:	cost of admissions to number of customers	sales tax to Ocean Bike Tours price	distance to time traveled by cyclist
Equation:	$c = 21n$	$T = 0.06P$	$d = 20t$

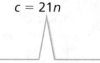
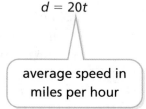

Description of Coefficient:	price per customer	tax rate per dollar	average speed in miles per hour

Relationships with rules in the form $y = mx$ occur often. It is important to understand the patterns in tables and graphs that those relationships produce. It is also useful to understand the special information provided in each case by m—the coefficient of x.

In these equations, the coefficient tells the **rate of change** in the dependent variable as the independent variable increases steadily.

 How is the rate of change represented in an equation, table, and graph?

The questions in this Problem will develop your understanding and skill in working with rates in many different situations.

Problem 3.2

A When the bike tour is over, the riders will put their bikes and gear into vans and head back to Atlantic City.

1. Copy and complete the rate table to show how distance depends on time for different average speeds.

Distance Traveled at Different Average Speeds

Time (h)	Distance for Speed of 50 mi/h	Distance for Speed of 55 mi/h	Distance for Speed of 60 mi/h
0	0	▨	▨
1	50	▨	▨
2	100	▨	▨
3	▨	▨	▨
4	▨	▨	▨

2. Write an equation to show how distance *d* and time *t* are related for travel at each speed.

   a. 50 miles per hour

   b. 55 miles per hour

   c. 60 miles per hour

3. Graph the (*time, distance*) data for all three speeds on the same coordinate grid. Use a different color for each speed.

4. For each of the three average speeds:

   a. Look for patterns relating distance and time in the table and graph. Explain how the pattern shows up in the table and graph.

   b. Theo observed that the coefficient of the independent variable in each equation is the average speed or unit rate. Is he correct? Explain.

5. **a.** Explain how you can use the table, graph, or equation to find the distance when *t* = 6 hours.

   b. How can you use the table, graph, or equation to find the time when the distance is 275 miles? Explain.

continued on the next page >

Problem 3.2 *continued*

B A smartphone plan charges $.03 per text message.

1. a. Make a table of monthly charges for 0; 500; 1,000; 1,500; 2,000; and 2,500 text messages.

   b. Use the table. What is the cost for 1,000 messages? For 1,725 messages?

   c. Use the table. How many text messages were sent in a month if the charge for the messages is $75? $60? $18?

2. a. How is the monthly charge *B* for text messages related to the number of text messages *n*? Write an equation that represents the monthly charge for *n* messages.

   b. Use the equation you wrote in part (a) to find the cost for 1,250 text messages in one month.

3. a. Sketch a graph of the relationship between text message charges and number of messages.

   b. Explain how you could use the graph to answer the questions in parts (1b), (1c), and (2b).

C The metric and English system units for measuring length are related. The rule is that 1 inch is equal to about 2.5 centimeters.

1. What is the length in centimeters of a line segment that has measure 5 inches? 12 inches? 7.5 inches?

2. How can you calculate the length in centimeters *C* of an object that you have measured in inches *I*? Write an equation to represent this calculation. Use the equation to find the number of centimeters that corresponds to 12 inches.

3. What is the approximate length in inches of a line segment that has measure 10 centimeters? 30 centimeters? 100 centimeters?

4. Sketch a graph of the relationship between length in centimeters and length in inches in part (2). Explain how you could use the graph to answer the questions in parts (1) and (3).

Problem 3.2 *continued*

D The equations you wrote in Questions A–C all have the form $y = mx$.

1. For each equation below, make a table of (x, y) values. Use whole-number values of x from 0 to 6. Then use your table to make a graph.

   a. $y = 2x$ **b.** $y = 0.5x$ **c.** $y = 1.5x$ **d.** $y = x$

2. Explain the connection between the number m and the pattern in the table of values and graph of $y = mx$.

3. **a.** Explain how you can find the value of y using a table, graph, or equation if $x = 2$.

   b. Explain how you can find the value of x using a table, graph or equation if $y = 6$.

4. Write a story to represent each equation in part (1).

E What similarities and differences do you find in the equations, tables, and graphs for the relationships in Questions A–D?

A C E Homework starts on page 76.

3.3 Group Discounts and a Bonus Card
Equations With Two Operations

Each equation you wrote in Problems 3.1 and 3.2 involved only one operation $(+, -, \times, \div)$. Some equations involve two or more arithmetic operations. To write such equations, you can reason just as you do with one-operation equations:

- Identify the variables.

- Work out some specific numeric examples. Examine them carefully. Then, look for patterns in the calculations used.

- Write a rule in words to describe the general pattern in the calculations.

- Convert your rule to an equation with letter variables and symbols.

- Think about whether your equation makes sense. Test it for a few values to see if it works.

Problem 3.3

Liz and Theo want to visit Wild World with their friends. Theo checks if the park offers special prices for groups larger than 3 people. He finds this information on the park's Web site:

Wild World AMUSEMENT PARK

Regular Admission
$21.00 per person

Includes 100-point **BONUS CARD**

Special Group Price
$50.00 plus $10.00 per group member

A Study the rule.

1. a. Make a table to show the admission price for groups of size 4, 8, 12, 16, 20, 24, 28, 32, 36, and 40 people. Then sketch a graph of the data.

   b. Describe the pattern of change that shows up in the table and graph.

2. a. Describe in words how you can calculate the admission price for a group with any number of people.

   b. Write an equation relating admission price p to group size n.

   c. How is this pattern of change in prices for group admissions similar to the pattern of change for the equations in Problem 3.2? How is it different?

3. a. Describe how you can use the table, graph, or equation to find the cost for 18 people.

   b. Describe how you can use the table or graph to find the number of people in the group if the total charge is $350 or $390.

Problem **3.3** | *continued*

B Admission to Wild World includes a bonus card with 100 points that can be spent on rides. Rides cost 6 points each.

  1. Copy and complete the table below to show a customer's bonus card balance after various numbers of rides.

Bonus Card Balance

Number of Rides	0	1	2	3	5	7	10	15
Points on Card	100	■	■	■	■	■	■	■

  2. Explain how you can calculate the number of points left after any number of rides.

  3. Write an equation showing the relationship between points left on the bonus card and number of rides taken.

  4. How does cost per ride appear in the equation? How does the number of bonus points at the start appear in the equation?

  5. Sketch a graph of the relationship between points left and number of rides for up to 20 rides. Describe the relationship between the variables.

C Liz wonders whether they should rent a cart to carry their backpacks. The equation $c = 20 + 5h$ shows the cost in dollars c of renting a cart for h hours.

  1. What information does each number and variable in the expression $20 + 5h$ represent?

  2. Use the equation to make a table showing the cost of renting a cart for 0, 1, 2, 3, 4, 5, and 6 hours. Then make a graph of the data.

  3. Explain how the cost per hour shows up in the table, graph, and equation.

  4. Explain how the 20 in the equation is represented in the table and in the graph.

  5. Which of the following points satisfy the relationship represented by the equation? (0, 4), (0, 20), (7, 55) Explain your reasoning.

A C E Homework starts on page 76.

3.4 Getting the Calculation Right
Expressions and Order of Operations

The equation $p = 50 + 10n$ represents the relationship between the Wild World admission price p in dollars and the number of people n in a group. The right side of the equation $50 + 10n$ is an algebraic expression. It represents the value of the dependent variable, p. It involves two operations, addition and multiplication.

The critical question is, 'Which operation comes first?'

Theo wants to find the admission price for an Ocean Bike Tours group with 17 members. He first works from left to right:

$$50 + 10 \times 17$$
$$= 60 \times 17$$
$$= 1{,}020$$

He gets a number that seems too large.

Then Theo enters the same expression on his calculator and gets:

$$50 + 10*17 = 220$$

He is puzzled by the difference in results. Then Theo remembers that there are rules for evaluating expressions.

- Which is the correct answer? Why?

Here are the rules known as the Order of Operations:

1. Work within parentheses.
2. Write numbers written with exponents in standard form.
3. Do all multiplication and division in order from left to right.
4. Do all addition and subtraction in order from left to right.

Use the Order of Operations with $7 + (6 \times 4 - 9) \div 3$.

$$7 + (6 \times 4 - 9) \div 3 = 7 + (24 - 9) \div 3$$
$$= 7 + (15) \div 3$$
$$= 7 + 5$$
$$= 12$$

Problem 3.4

Practice the Order of Operations rules on these examples.

A The group admission price at Wild World is given by the equation $p = 50 + 10n$. Find the prices for groups with 5, 11, and 23 members.

B The equation $b = 100 - 6r$ gives the number of points left on a Wild World bonus card after r rides. Find the numbers of points left after 3, 7, and 14 rides.

C Celia makes plans for the van ride home to Atlantic City from Williamsburg. She plans for a 2-hour stop in Baltimore, Maryland. To predict trip time t from average driving speed s, she writes the equation

$$t = 2 + \frac{350}{s}$$

Find the predicted trip times for average driving speeds of 45, 55, and 65 miles per hour.

D Sidney writes two equations: $I = 350n$ and $E = 150n + 1000$. The equations relate income I and operating expenses E to number of customers.

Sidney writes the equation $P = 350n - (150n + 1000)$ to show how tour profit P depends on the number of customers n. Use the rule to find profits P for 8, 12, 20, and 30 customers.

E The Ocean Bike Tours partners have an Atlantic City workshop in the shape of a cube. The formula for the surface area of a cube is $A = 6s^2$. The formula for the volume of a cube is $V = s^3$.

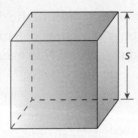

Area $= 6s^2$
Volume $= s^3$

1. If each edge of the cubical workshop is 4.25 meters long, what is the total surface area of the floor, walls, and ceiling?

2. What is the volume of the workshop?

A C E Homework starts on page 76.

Applications

1.   **a.** Natasha charges $12 per hour for babysitting in her neighborhood. What equation relates her pay for a job to the number of hours she works?

   b. A gasoline service station offers 20 cents off the regular price per gallon every Tuesday. What equation relates the discounted price to the regular price on that day?

   c. Write an equation to show how the perimeter of a square is related to the length of a side of the square.

   d. A middle school wants to have its students see a movie at a local theater. The total cost of the theater and movie rental is $1,500. What equation shows how the cost per student depends on the number of students who attend?

2.   Celia writes the equation $d = 8t$ to represent the distance in miles d that riders could travel in t hours at a speed of 8 miles per hour. Make a table that shows the distance traveled every half hour, up to 5 hours, if riders travel at this constant speed.

3. A girls' basketball team is playing in the Texas state championship game. They are going 560 miles from El Paso to San Antonio. Their bus travels at an average speed of 60 miles per hour.

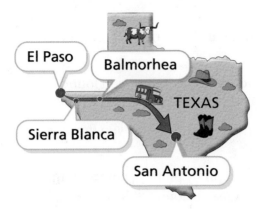

a. Suppose the bus travels at an almost steady speed throughout the trip. Make a table and a graph of time and distance data for the bus.

b. Estimate the distance the bus travels in 2 hours, $2\frac{3}{4}$ hours, $3\frac{1}{2}$ hours, and 7.25 hours.

c. Describe in words and with an equation a rule you could use to calculate the distance traveled for any given time on this trip.

d. The bus route passes through Sierra Blanca, which is 90 miles from El Paso. About how long does it take the bus to get to Sierra Blanca?

e. The bus route also passes through Balmorhea, which is $\frac{1}{3}$ of the way from El Paso to San Antonio. About how long does it take the bus to get to Balmorhea?

f. How long does it take the bus to complete its 560-mile trip to San Antonio?

g. Explain in words and with an equation how time t for the 560-mile trip depends on average speed s.

h. Use the rule from part (g) to calculate trip time if the average bus speed is 50 miles per hour, 45 miles per hour, and 70 miles per hour.

4. The equation $d = 70t$ represents the distance in miles covered after traveling at 70 miles per hour for t hours.

   a. Make a table that shows the distance traveled every half hour from 0 hours to 4 hours.

   b. Sketch a coordinate graph that shows the distance traveled between 0 and 4 hours.

   c. What is d when $t = 2.5$ hours? Explain how you found your answer.

   d. What is t when $d = 210$ miles? Explain how you found your answer.

   e. You probably made your graph by plotting points. In this situation, would it make sense to connect these points?

5. The table shows the relationship between the number of riders on a bike tour and the daily cost of providing box lunches.

Bike Tour Box Lunch Costs

Number of Riders	1	2	3	4	5	6	7	8	9
Lunch Cost	$4.25	$8.50	$12.75	$17.00	$21.25	$25.50	$29.75	$34.00	$38.25

   a. Explain in words and with an equation how lunch cost L depends on the number of riders n.

   b. Use your equation to find the lunch cost for 25 riders.

   c. How many riders could eat lunch for $89.25? Explain how you found your answer.

For Exercises 6–8, use the equation to complete the table.

6. $y = 4x + 3$

x	1	2	5	10	20	■
y	■	■	■	■	■	203

7. $m = 100 - k$

k	1	2	5	10	20	■
m	■	■	■	■	■	50

8. $d = 3.5t$

t	1	2	5	10	20	■
d	■	■	■	■	■	140

9. Sean plans to buy a new tablet for $315. The store offers him an interest-free payment plan that allows him to pay in monthly installments of $25.

Great buy! TABLETS

BUY NOW PAY LATER

Monthly Installments of **$25**

NO DEPOSIT • NO INTEREST

a. How much will Sean still owe after one payment? After two payments? After three payments?

b. Explain in words how the amount owed depends on the number of payments made. Then write an equation for calculating the amount owed *a* for any number of payments *n*.

c. Use your equation to make a table and graph showing the relationship between *n* and *a*.

d. As *n* increases by 1, how does *a* change? How is this change shown in the table? How is it shown on the graph?

e. How many payments will Sean have to make in all? How is this shown in the table? How is it shown on the graph?

For Exercises 10–13, express each rule with an equation. Use single letters to stand for the variables. Identify what each letter represents.

10. The area of a rectangle is its length multiplied by its width.

11. The number of hot dogs needed for a picnic is two for each student.

12. The amount of material needed to make curtains is 4 square yards per window.

13. Taxi fare is $2.00 plus $1.10 per mile.

14. The sales tax in a state is 8%. Write an equation for the amount of tax t on an item that costs d dollars.

15. Potatoes sell for $.25 per pound at the produce market. Write an equation for the cost c of p pounds of potatoes.

16. A cellphone family plan costs $49 per month plus $.05 per text. Write an equation for the monthly bill b when t texts are sent.

For Exercises 17–19, describe the relationship between the variables in words and with an equation.

17.

x	0	1	2	5	10	20
y	0	4	8	20	40	80

18.

s	0	1	2	3	6	12
t	50	49	48	47	44	38

19.

n	0	1	2	3	4	5
z	1	6	11	16	21	26

20. Multiple Choice Which equation describes the relationship in the table?

n	0	1	2	3	4	5	6
C	10	20	30	40	50	60	70

A. $C = 10n$

B. $C = 10 + n$

C. $C = 10$

D. $C = 10 + 10n$

21. Use the Order of Operations to evaluate each algebraic expression when $n = 5$ and when $n = 10$.

a. $3n - 12$

b. $45 - 3n$

c. $7(4n + 2) - 8$

d. $3(n - 4)^2 + 9$

Connections

22. **a.** The perimeter P of a square is related to the side length s by the formula $P = 4s$.

    Make a table showing how the perimeter of a square increases as the side length increases from 1 to 6 in 1-unit steps. Describe the pattern of change.

    b. The area A of a square is related to the side length by the formula $A = s^2$.

    Add a row to the table in part (a) to show how the area of the square increases as the side length increases. Describe the pattern of change.

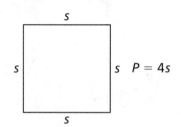

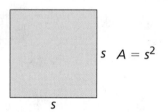

For Exercises 23–25, find the indicated value or values.

23. the tenth odd number (1 is the first odd number, 3 is the second odd number, and so on.)

24. the area of a triangle with a base of 10 centimeters and a height of 15 centimeters

25. $3^3 \times 5^2 \times 7$

For Exercises 26–30, write a formula for the given quantity.

26. the area A of a rectangle with length l and width w

27. the area A of a parallelogram with base b and height h

28. the perimeter P of a rectangle with base b and height h

29. the nth odd number, O (1 is the first odd number, 3 is the second odd number, and so on.)

30. the area A of a triangle with base b and height h

For Exercises 31 and 32, copy and complete the table of values for the given equation.

31. a. $y = x + \frac{1}{2}$

x	$\frac{1}{5}$	$\frac{1}{4}$	$\frac{1}{3}$	$\frac{2}{5}$	$\frac{1}{2}$	$\frac{2}{3}$	$\frac{3}{4}$	5
y	▦	▦	▦	▦	▦	▦	▦	▦

b. $y = x - \frac{1}{2}$

x	$\frac{1}{2}$	$\frac{2}{3}$	$\frac{3}{4}$	1	$1\frac{1}{2}$	2	3	4
y	▦	▦	▦	▦	▦	▦	▦	▦

32. a. $y = \frac{1}{2}x$

x	$\frac{1}{5}$	$\frac{1}{4}$	$\frac{1}{3}$	$\frac{2}{5}$	$\frac{1}{2}$	$\frac{2}{3}$	$\frac{3}{4}$	5
y	▦	▦	▦	▦	▦	▦	▦	▦

b. $y = \frac{1}{2} \div x$

x	$\frac{1}{5}$	$\frac{1}{4}$	$\frac{1}{3}$	$\frac{2}{5}$	$\frac{1}{2}$	$\frac{2}{3}$	$\frac{3}{4}$	5
y	▦	▦	▦	▦	▦	▦	▦	▦

For Exercises 33–35, describe in words the relationship between x and y.

33.

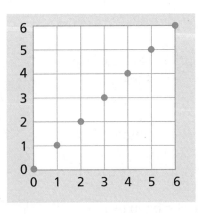

34.

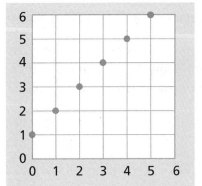

35.

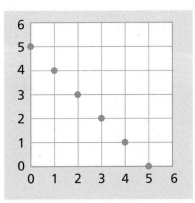

Extensions

36. You can calculate the average speed of a car trip if you know the distance and time traveled.

    a. Copy and complete the table below.

Car Trips

Distance (mi)	Time (h)	Average Speed (mi/h)
145	2	▪
110	2	▪
165	2.5	▪
300	5.25	▪
446	6.75	▪
528	8	▪

    b. Write a formula for calculating the average speed s for any given distance d and time t.

For Exercises 37–40, solve by estimating and checking.

37. The equation $p = 50 + 10n$ gives the admission price p to Wild World for a group of n people. A club's budget has $500 set aside for a visit to the park. How many club members can go?

38. The equation $b = 100 - 6r$ gives the number of bonus points b left on a Wild World bonus card after r rides.

    a. Rosi has 34 points left. How many rides has she been on?

    b. Dwight has 16 points left. How many rides has he been on?

39. The equation $d = 2.5t$ describes the distance in meters d covered by a canoe-racing team in t seconds. How long does it take the team to go 125 meters? 400 meters?

40. The equation $d = 400 - 2.5t$ describes the distance in meters d of a canoe-racing team from the finish line t seconds after a race starts. When is the team 175 meters from the finish line? 100 meters from the finish line?

41. Armen builds models from rods. When he builds bridges, he makes the sides using patterns of triangles like the ones below. The total number of rods depends on the number of rods along the bottom.

Rods along bottom = 3

Total number of rods = 11

Rods along bottom = 4

Total number of rods = 15

a. Copy and complete the table.

Rod Bridges

Rods Along the Bottom	1	2	3	4	5	6	7	8	9	10
Total Number of Rods	3	7	11	▪	▪	▪	▪	▪	▪	▪

b. Write an equation relating the total number of rods t to the number of rods along the bottom b. Explain how the formula you write relates to the way Armen puts the rods together.

c. For the design below, make a table and write an equation relating the total number of rods t to the number of rods along the bottom b.

42. The Ocean Bike Tours partners decided to include a visit to Wild World Amusement Park as part of the tour. These are the cost and income factors:

WE HAVE AN <u>INCOME</u> OF $350 PER PERSON.

List of Costs:

- $30 per person for bike rental
- $125 per person for food and campsites
- $700 for van rental
- $50 plus $10 per person for Wild World Admission
- $25 per person for buses to return riders from Williamsburg to Atlantic City

a. Combining all of these factors, what equation relates expected tour profit P to the number of customers n who take the trip?

b. For what number of customers will a tour group produce profit greater than $500?

In this Investigation, you wrote algebraic equations to express relationships between variables. You analyzed the relationships using tables and graphs. You also related the tables and graphs to the equations you wrote. The following questions will help you summarize what you have learned.

Think about these questions. Discuss your ideas with other students and your teacher. Then write a summary of your findings in your notebook.

1. **What** strategies help in finding equations to express relationships?

2. For relationships given by equations in the form $y = mx$:

   a. **How** does the value of y change as the value of x increases?

   b. **How** is the pattern of change shown in a table, graph, and equation of the function?

3. a. In this Unit, you have represented relationships between variables with tables, graphs, and equations. **List** some advantages and disadvantages of each of these representations.

   b. If the value of one variable in a relationship is known, **describe** how you can use a table, graph, or equation to find a value of the other variable.

Common Core Mathematical Practices

As you worked on the Problems in this Investigation, you used prior knowledge to make sense of them. You also applied Mathematical Practices to solve the Problems. Think back over your work, the ways you thought about the Problems, and how you used Mathematical Practices.

Tori described her thoughts in the following way:

We looked for patterns among the graphs and equations in Problem 3.1.

We noticed something about the graphs for the equations of the form $y = mx$. They all contained the point $(1, m)$. Kelly said that m is also the unit rate.

Common Core Standards for Mathematical Practice

MP8 Look for and express regularity in repeated reasoning.

 • What other Mathematical Practices can you identify in Tori's reasoning?

• Describe a Mathematical Practice that you and your classmates used to solve a different Problem in this Investigation.

Expressions, Equations, and Inequalities

Working on Investigation 3 developed your skill in writing expressions for relationships between independent and dependent variables. The Problems of this Investigation deal with three more questions about such relationships between variables:

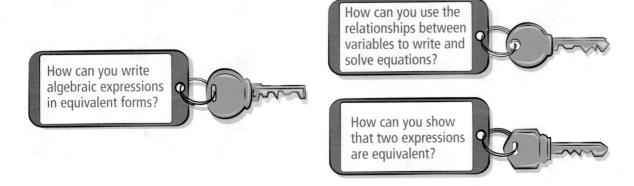

How can you use the relationships between variables to write and solve equations?

How can you write algebraic expressions in equivalent forms?

How can you show that two expressions are equivalent?

Answers to these questions are key ideas of algebra.

....

Common Core State Standards

6.EE.A.3 Apply the properties of operations to generate equivalent expressions.

6.EE.B.5 Understand solving an equation or inequality as a process of answering a question: which values from a specified set, if any, make the equation or inequality true? Use substitution to determine whether a given number in a specified set makes an equation or inequality true.

6.EE.B.7 Solve real-world and mathematical problems by writing and solving equations of the form $x + p = q$ and $px = q$ for cases in which p, q and x are all nonnegative rational numbers.

6.EE.B.8 Write an inequality of the form $x > c$ or $x < c$ to represent a constraint or condition in a real-world or mathematical problem. Recognize that inequalities of the form $x > c$ or $x < c$ have infinitely many solutions; represent solutions of such inequalities on number line diagrams.

Also 6.RP.A.3a, 6.RP.A.3b, 6.EE.A.2, 6.EE.A.2a, 6.EE.A.2b, 6.EE.A.2c, 6.EE.A.4, 6.EE.B.6, 6.EE.C.9

4.1 Taking the Plunge
Equivalent Expressions I

One of the most popular rides at Wild World is the Sky Dive. Riders are lifted in a car 250 feet in the air. When the car is released, it falls back to the ground. It reaches a speed near 50 miles per hour.

The riders' seats are around a tower that looks like a stack of cubes made from steel pieces. Each face of the Sky Dive tower looks like a ladder of squares.

Tower

Ladder

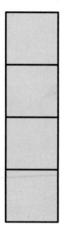

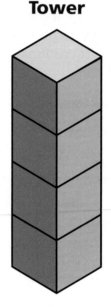

- How many steel pieces do you need to build each of these figures?

Suppose that you were building the tower for a similar ride.

- How many steel pieces would you need to make a ladder of *n* squares?

- How many steel pieces would you need to make a tower of *n* cubes?

As you work on these questions, it might help to make some model ladders using toothpicks.

Problem 4.1

A 1. Look at the ladder of squares. What numbers would go in the second row of this table?

Number of Squares	1	2	3	4	5	10	20
Number of Pieces	4	■	■	■	■	■	■

2. Write an equation that shows how to find the number of pieces *P* needed to make a ladder of *n* squares.

B 1. Look at the tower of cubes. What numbers would go in the second row of a table that counts steel pieces needed to make a tower of *n* cubes?

Number of Cubes	1	2	3	4	5	10	20
Number of Pieces	12	■	■	■	■	■	■

2. Write an equation that shows how to find the number of steel pieces in a tower of *n* cubes.

ACE Homework starts on page 100.

4.2 More Than One Way to Say It

Equivalent Expressions II

A group of students worked on the ladder problem. Four of them came up with equations relating the number of steel pieces P to the number of squares n.

> Tabitha: $P = n + n + n + 1$ Chaska: $P = 1 + 3n$
>
> Latrell: $P = 4n$ Eva: $P = 4 + 3(n - 1)$

Recall that groups of mathematical symbols such as $n + n + n + 1$, $1 + 3n$, $4n$, and $4 + 3(n - 1)$ are called *algebraic expressions*. Each expression represents the value of the dependent variable P. When two expressions give the same results for every value of the variable, they are called **equivalent expressions.**

? Which expressions for P are equivalent? Explain why.

Problem 4.2

A **1.** What thinking might have led the students to their ideas?

2. Do the four equations predict the same numbers of steel pieces for ladders of any height n? Test your ideas by comparing values of P when $n = 1, 5, 10$, and 20.

3. Which of the expressions for the number of steel pieces in a ladder of n squares are equivalent? Explain why.

4. Are any of the expressions equivalent to your own from Problem 4.1? How can you be sure?

B **1.** Think about building a tower of cubes. Write two more expressions that are equivalent to the expression you wrote in part (2) of Question B in Problem 4.1. Explain why they are equivalent.

2. Pick two equivalent expressions from part (1). Use them to generate a table and graph for each. Compare the tables and graphs.

A C E Homework starts on page 100.

4.3 Putting It All Together
Equivalent Expressions III

In an expression such as $1 + 3n$, the 1 and the $3n$ are called **terms** of the expression. In the expression $4 + 3(n - 1)$ there are 2 terms, 4 and $3(n - 1)$. Note that the expression $(n - 1)$ is both a factor of the term $3(n - 1)$ and a difference of two terms. The 3 is the **coefficient** of n in the expression $1 + 3n$.

The Distributive Property helps to show that two expressions are equivalent. It states that for any numbers a, b, and c the following is true:

$$a(b + c) = ab + ac$$

This means that:

- A number can be expressed both as a product and as a sum.

- The area of a rectangle can be found in two different ways.

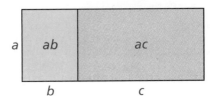

The expression $a(b + c)$ is in *factored form*.

The expression $a(b) + a(c)$ is in *expanded form*.

The expressions $a(b + c)$ and $ab + ac$ are *equivalent expressions*.

- Use the Distributive Property to write an equivalent expression for $5x + 6x$.

- How does this help write an equivalent expression for $n + n + n + 1$?

With their plans almost complete, the Ocean Bike Tours partners have made a list of tour operating costs.

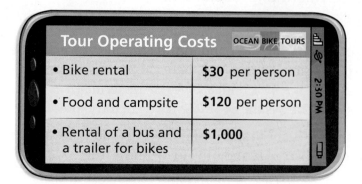

Tour Operating Costs	OCEAN BIKE TOURS
• Bike rental	**$30** per person
• Food and campsite	**$120** per person
• Rental of a bus and a trailer for bikes	**$1,000**

• What equation can represent the total costs?

• Is there more than one possible equation? Explain.

Problem 4.3

The next step in planning is to write these costs as algebraic expressions.

(A) What equations show how the three cost variables depend on the number of riders n?

1. bike rental $B =$ ▩

2. food and campsite fees $F =$ ▩

3. rental of the bus and trailer $R =$ ▩

(B) Three of the business partners write equations that relate total tour cost C to the number of riders n:

> Celia's equation: $C = 30n + 120n + 1000$
>
> Theo's equation: $C = 150n + 1000$
>
> Liz's equation: $C = 1150n$

1. **a.** Are any or all of these equations correct? If so, are they equivalent? Explain why.

   b. For the equations that are correct, explain what information each term and coefficient represents in the equation.

Problem **4.3** *continued*

2. Compare the equations. Use Order of Operations guidelines to complete the table below of sample (n, C) values. What does the table suggest about which expressions for C are equivalent?

Operating Cost Related to Number of Customers

Number of Customers n	5	10	15	20	25
$C = 30n + 120n + 1000$	▪	▪	▪	▪	▪
$C = 150n + 1000$	▪	▪	▪	▪	▪
$C = 1150n$	▪	▪	▪	▪	▪

3. What results would you expect if you were to graph the three equations below?

$$C = 30n + 120n + 1000$$

$$C = 150n + 1000$$

$$C = 1150n$$

Check your ideas by graphing.

4. Use properties of operations such as the Distributive Property to show which expressions for cost are equivalent.

C **1.** For each expression below, list the terms and the coefficient in each term.

 a. $5x + x + 6$ **b.** $10q - 2q$

2. Use the properties of operations to write an equivalent expression for each expression above.

3. Show that $1 + 3n = 4 + 3(n - 1)$.

D Sidney points out that all three partners left out the cost of the Wild World Amusement Park trip. The cost for that part of the tour is $W = 50 + 10n$. How does this cost factor change each correct equation?

A C E Homework starts on page 100.

4.4 Finding the Unknown Value
Solving Equations

The Ocean Bike Tours partners decide to charge $350 per rider.
This leads them to an equation giving tour income I for n riders: $I = 350n$.
You can use the equation to find the income for 10 riders.

$$I = 350n$$

$$I = 350 \times 10$$

$$I = 3{,}500$$

Suppose you are asked to find the number of riders needed to reach a tour income goal of $4,200. In earlier work you used tables and graphs to estimate answers. You can also use the equation: $4{,}200 = 350n$.

Solving the equation means finding values of n that makes the equation $4{,}200 = 350n$ a true statement. Any values of n that work are called **solutions of the equation.**

One way to solve equations is to think about the fact families that relate arithmetic operations. Examples:

$5 + 7 = 12$
$5 = 12 - 7$

> Both equations describe true relationships between 5, 7, and 12.

$5(7) = 35$
$5 = 35 \div 7$

> Both equations describe true relationships between 5, 7, and 35.

- How are fact families helpful to solve equations such as $c = 350n$?

When you find the solution of an equation, it is always a good idea to check your work.

Is $n = 12$ a solution for $4{,}200 = 35n$?

    Substitute 12 for n: $4{,}200 = 35(12)$.

Is this a true statement?

    Multiplying 35 by 12 equals 4,200.

Yes, 12 is the solution.

Problem 4.4

(A) Single admissions at Wild World Amusement Park cost $21. If the park sells n single admissions in one day, its income is $I = 21n$.

1. Write an equation to answer this question:
   How many single admissions were sold on a day the park had income of $9,450 from single admissions?

2. Solve the equation. Explain how you found your answer.

3. How can you check your answer?

(B) On the Ocean Bike Tours test run, Sidney stopped the van at a gas station. The station advertised 25 cents off per gallon on Tuesdays.

1. Write an equation for the Tuesday discount price d. Use p as the price on other days.

2. Use the equation to find the price on days other than Tuesday if the discount price is $2.79.

(C) Ocean Bike Tours wants to provide bandanas for each person. The cost of the bandanas is $95.50 for the design plus $1 per bandana.

1. Write an equation that represents this relationship.

2. Use the equation to find the cost for 50 bandanas.

3. Use the equation to find the number bandanas if the total cost is $116.50.

In Questions A–C you wrote and solved equations that match questions about the bike tour. Knowing about the problem situation often helps in writing and solving equations. But the methods you use in those cases can be applied to other equations without stories to help your reasoning.

(D) Use ideas you've learned about solving equations to solve the equations below. Show your calculations. Check each solution in the equation.

1. $x + 22.5 = 49.25$

2. $37.2 = n - 12$

3. $55t = 176$

A C E Homework starts on page 100.

4.5 It's Not Always Equal
Solving Inequalities

In each part of Problem 4.4 you wrote and solved an equation about Ocean Bike Tours. For example, you wrote the equation $21I = C$. Then you were told that income was \$9,450. You solved the equation $21I = 9,450$ to find the number of riders. The solution was $I = 450$.

Suppose you were asked a related question: How many single-admission sales will bring income of more than \$9,450?

To answer this question, you need to solve the inequality $21I > 9,450$. That is, you need to find values of the variable I that make the given inequality true. This task is very similar to what you did when comparing rental plans offered by the two bike shops in Problem 2.1.

If $21I = 9,450$, then $I = 450$. So, any number $I > 450$ is a solution to the inequality $21I > 9,450$. A graph of these solutions on a number line is:

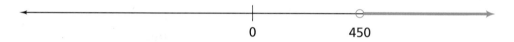

0   450

- What are five possible solutions for I?

- What are five more possible solutions for I?

- How many possible solutions does this inequality have?

In general, the solution to a simple inequality can be written in the form $x > c$ or $x < c$. Those solutions can be graphed on a number line. Below are two examples.

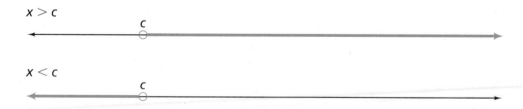

$x > c$

c

$x < c$

c

- What does the thicker part of each number line tell you about solutions to the inequality?

Problem 4.5

Use what you know about variables, expressions, and equations to write and solve inequalities that match Questions A–C. In each case, do the following.

- Write an inequality that helps to answer the question.

- Give at least 3 specific number solutions to the inequality. Then explain why they work.

- Describe all possible solutions.

A The bungee jump at Wild World charges $35. How many jumpers are needed for the jump to earn income of more than $1,050 in a day?

B A gas station sign says regular unleaded gasoline costs $4 per gallon. How much gas can Mike buy if he has $17.50 in his pocket?

C Ocean Bike Tours wants to provide bandanas for each customer. The costs are $95.50 for the design plus $1 per bandana. How many bandanas can they buy if they want the cost to be less than $400?

D Use ideas about solving equations and inequalities from Questions A, B, and C to solve the inequalities below.

   1. $84 < 14m$

   2. $55t > 176$

   3. $x + 22.5 < 49.25$

   4. $37.2 > n - 12$

E Draw number lines to graph the solutions to all inequalities in Question D.

F **1.** Make up a problem that can be represented by the equation $y = 50 + 4x$.

   2. Which of these points lie on the graph of the equation? (8, 92), (15, 110)

   3. Use a point that lies on the graph to make up a question that the point can answer.

   4. Use a point that lies on the graph to write an inequality that the point satisfies.

A C E Homework starts on page 100.

Applications

For Exercises 1–3, use the toothpick patterns created by Scott, Ahna, and Lloyd.

1. Scott's Pattern

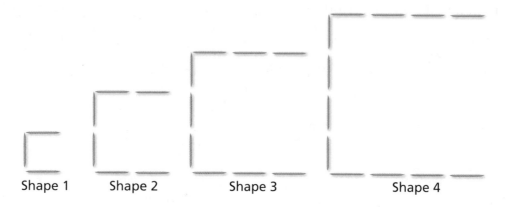

Shape 1 Shape 2 Shape 3 Shape 4

a. Look at the table comparing the shape number to the number of toothpicks. What numbers go in the second row?

Shape Number	4	5	6	7	8	10	20
Number of Toothpicks	12	■	■	■	■	■	■

b. What equation shows how to find the number of toothpicks needed for shape number *n*?

c. Is there a different equation you could write for part (b)?

2. Ahna's Pattern

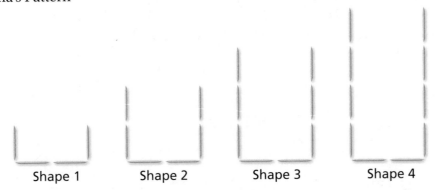

Shape 1   Shape 2   Shape 3   Shape 4

a. What numbers go in the second row of the table comparing the shape number to the number of toothpicks?

Shape Number	4	5	6	7	8	10	20
Number of Toothpicks	10	■	■	■	■	■	■

b. What equation shows how to find the number of toothpicks needed for shape number n?

c. How are Ahna and Scott's Patterns similar or different?

3. Lloyd's Pattern

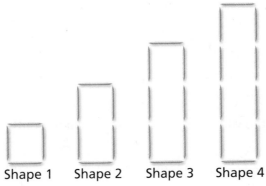

Shape 1   Shape 2   Shape 3   Shape 4

a. What numbers go in the second row of a table comparing the shape number to the number of toothpicks?

Shape Number	4	5	6	7	8	10	20
Number of Toothpicks	10	■	■	■	■	■	■

b. What equation shows the number of toothpicks needed for shape number n?

c. How is the relationship between Lloyd and Ahna's Patterns similar or different?

4. Wild World is designing a giant swing using a structure built in much the same way as the Sky Dive in Problem 4.1. The designers are not sure how tall to make the swing. Here are some sketches of different swing designs.

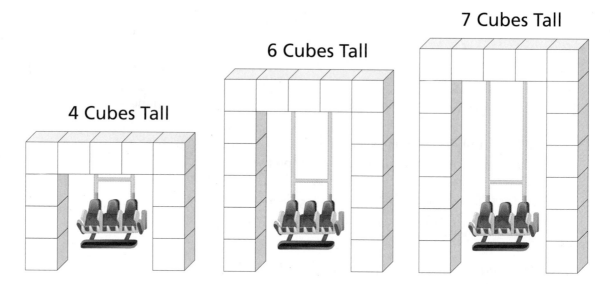

7 Cubes Tall

6 Cubes Tall

4 Cubes Tall

a. What numbers would go in the second row of a table that compares the height to the total number of cubes?

Height (squares)	4	5	6	7	8	10	20
Number of Cubes	11	▦	▦	▦	▦	▦	▦

b. What equation shows how to find the number of cubes in the swing frame that is *n* cubes tall?

c. Could you calculate the value for a swing frame that is 1 cube tall? Explain.

d. Explain what a swing frame that is 50 cubes tall would look like. In what ways would it look similar to and different from the swing frames shown above? How could you use this description to calculate the total number of cubes in it?

5. Mitch, Lewis, and Corky were discussing equations that they wrote for Exercise 4. They called the height T and the number of cubes c.

Mitch's thinking: The top of the swing frame has 5 cubes, and then there are $T - 1$ cubes underneath it. The total number of cubes needed is $c = 5 + (T - 1) + (T - 1)$.

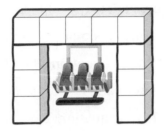

Lewis's thinking: When I see the drawing, I think of two upside-down L shapes with a middle piece. My equation for the number of cubes is $c = 2(T + 1) + 1$.

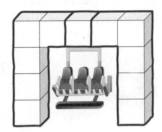

Corky's thinking: On the left side I see a single tower, and the right side is a tower with three extra cubes. My equation is $c = T + (T + 3)$.

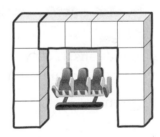

    a. Create a table for the three equations.

    b. Which of the expressions are equivalent? Explain.

    c. Write a new expression that is equivalent to the ones that are equivalent in part (b).

6. Students created some interesting expressions for Problem 4.2. They were not sure if these were equivalent to Chaska's, Tabitha's, and Eva's equations. Determine if each of the equations below is equivalent to the others.

   a. Martha's equation: $B = 2n + 2 + (n - 1)$

   b. Chad's equation: $B = 3(n + 1) - 2$

   c. Jeremiah's equation: $B = 4n - (n - 1)$

   d. Lara's equation: $B = 3 + 1n$

The Ocean Bike Tours partners decided to offer a two-day trip from Philadelphia, Pennsylvania, to Atlantic City, New Jersey, and back. They did some research and found these costs for the trip. Use the information shown below for Exercises 7–8.

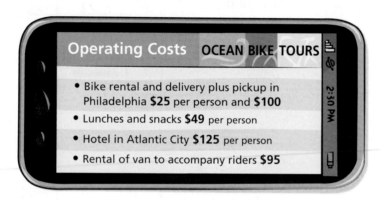

Operating Costs   OCEAN BIKE TOURS

- Bike rental and delivery plus pickup in Philadelphia **$25** per person and **$100**
- Lunches and snacks **$49** per person
- Hotel in Atlantic City **$125** per person
- Rental of van to accompany riders **$95**

2:30 PM

7. Write equations that show how these cost variables depend on the number n of customers for the two-day tours.

   a. bike rental B **b.** lunch and snacks L

   c. hotel rooms H **d.** rental of the tour support van V

8. **a.** Write a rule that shows how total operating cost C depends on the number n of riders. The rule should show how each cost variable adds to the total.

   b. Write another rule for total operating cost C. This rule should be as simple as possible for calculating the total cost.

   c. Give evidence showing that your two expressions for total cost are equivalent.

The organizers of a youth soccer league want to give each player a special T-shirt and hat. The costs are shown here.

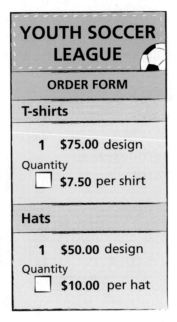

YOUTH SOCCER LEAGUE

ORDER FORM

T-shirts

1 $75.00 design

Quantity ☐ $7.50 per shirt

Hats

1 $50.00 design

Quantity ☐ $10.00 per hat

9. Show how the cost for each of the variables below depends on the number n of players in the tournament.

a. T-shirts T

b. hats H

10. a. Write an equation that shows how total cost C for providing T-shirts and hats depends on the number of tournament players n. The equation should show how each separate cost variable adds to the total.

b. Write a second equation for C. The second equation should be as simple as possible.

c. Give evidence to show that your two expressions for total cost are equivalent.

11. You are given the expression $350n - 30n + 350 - (50 + 10n)$.

a. What are the terms in the expression?

b. What numbers are coefficients in the expression?

c. Explain how the words *term* and *coefficient* are used in talking about the algebraic expression.

12. The owner of a horse farm has 500 yards of fencing to enclose a rectangular pasture. One side of the pasture must be 150 yards long. Write and solve an equation that tells the length of the other side.

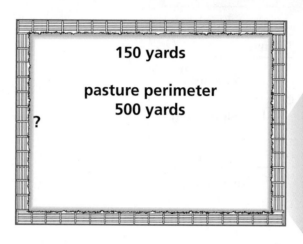

150 yards

pasture perimeter
500 yards

?

A baseball team wanted to rent a small bus for travel to a tournament. Superior Bus charges $2.95 per mile driven. Coast Transport charges $300 plus $2 per mile. Use these data for Exercises 13–16.

13. For each company, show how rental cost C depends on number of miles driven m.

14. The rental for a bus from Superior Bus was $590.

   • Write and solve an equation to find the distance driven.

   • Check your solution by substituting its value for the variable m in the equation.

   • Explain how you found the solution.

15. The rental for a bus from Coast Transport was $600.

   • Write and solve an equation to find the distance driven.

   • Check your solution by substituting its value for the variable m in the equation.

   • Explain how you found the solution.

16. The team wanted to know which bus company's offer was a better value. Use the table and graph below to answer their questions.

Miles	Superior Bus	Coast Transport
100	295	500
200	590	700
300	885	900
400	1180	1100
500	1475	1300

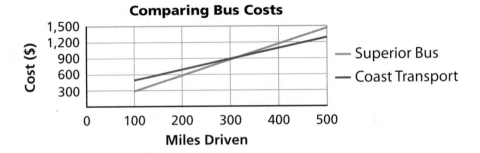

There are several ways to estimate solutions for equations.

The simplest method is often called **guess and check**. It involves three basic steps.

- Make a guess about the solution.

- Check to see if that guess solves the equation.

- If it does not, revise your guess and check again in the equation.

   a. The two rental companies charge the same amount for one distance. Write an equation to find that distance. Then solve the equation by guess and check. (The table and graph will help.)

   b. For what numbers of miles will the charge by Superior Bus be less than that by Coast Transport?

   c. For what numbers of miles will the charge by Coast Transport be less than that by Superior Buses?

The Ocean Bike Tours partners decided to charge $350 per rider. This led them to a relationship giving tour profit as $P = 190n - 1{,}050$. For 20 riders the profit will be $190(20) - 1{,}050 = 2{,}750$.

The partners want to find the number of riders needed to reach a profit of $3,700. They have to solve $3{,}700 = 190n - 1{,}050$. That means finding a value of n that makes $3{,}700 = 190n - 1{,}050$ a true statement.

Use the information below for Exercises 17–20.

17. Use the guess and check method to solve these equations. In each case write a sentence explaining what the solution tells about profit for Ocean Bike Tours.

   a. $3{,}700 = 190n - 1{,}050$.

   b. $550 = 190n - 1{,}050$

18. You can use a calculator or computer programs to help with guess and test solving. For example, here is a table of values for $P = 190n - 1050$.

Profit Related to Number of Customers

Number of Customers	5	10	15	20	25	30
Profit ($)	−100	850	1,800	2,750	3,700	4,650

   a. What do the entries in the table tell about solutions for the equation $1{,}230 = 190n - 1{,}050$?

   b. Use the table and the guess and check strategy to solve the equation.

   c. Use a table to help in solving these equations. In each case, write a sentence explaining what the solution tells about profit for Ocean Bike Tours.

   i. $2{,}560 = 190n - 1{,}050$ ii. $5{,}030 = 190n - 1{,}050$

19. Another version of the guess and test strategy uses graphs for the profit relationship.

   a. Study the graph below to estimate the value of n that is a solution for the equation $2,000 = 190n - 1,050$. Then check to see if your estimate is correct (or close to correct).

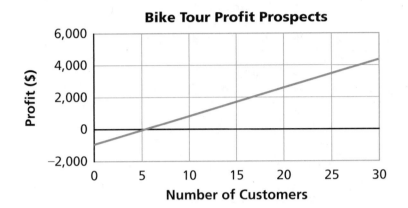

Bike Tour Profit Prospects

   b. Use graphing to solve these equations. In each case, sketch a graph and label points with coordinates that show the solution.

   i. $45 = 5x + 10$ **ii.** $60 = 100 - 2.5x$

20. The Ocean Bike Tours partners expect their profit P to depend on the number n of riders according to the relation $P = 190n - 1,050$.

   a. Use the relation to write an equation for the number of riders needed to give a profit of $2,180. Then solve the equation.

   b. What arithmetic operations give the solution?

Connections

For Exercises 21–24, use the pattern in each table to find the missing entries. Then write an equation relating the two variables.

21.

a	0	1	2	3	▪	8	20	100
b	0	7	14	21	28	▪	▪	▪

22.

x	0	1	2	3	4	8	20	100
y	6	7	8	9	▪	▪	▪	▪

23.

m	0	1	2	3	4	8	20	100
n	1	3	5	7	▪	▪	▪	▪

24.

r	0	1	2	3	4	6	10	20
s	0	1	4	9	16	▪	▪	▪

25. a. The table below shows the relationship between the number of cubes and number of squares in the tower. Use the information in Problem 4.1 to fill in the second row of the table.

Relationship of Cubes to Squares in a Tower

Number of Cubes in the Tower	1	2	3	4	5	6	10
Number of Squares in the Tower	▪	▪	▪	18	▪	▪	▪

b. What equation shows how to find the total number of squares *s* given the number of cubes *c*?

26. Determine if the pairs of expressions below are equivalent.
Explain how you know.

    a. $4n + 12$ and $4(n + 3)$

    b. $m + m + 3m$ and $3m + 2$

    c. $p + p$ and $p + 7$

    d. $5r + 5 - (r - 1)$ and $4r + 4$

    e. $3(2t + 2)$ and $(t + 1)6$

For Exercises 27–30 use what you know about equivalent expressions
to write an expression equivalent to the one given.

27. $5n$

28. $2n + 2$

29. $4n - 4$

30. $3n + 2n + n$

The diagrams in Exercises 31–34 show rectangles divided into smaller
rectangles. Use the Distributive Property to write two equivalent
expressions for the area of each large rectangle.

31.
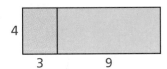

32.
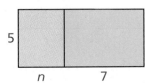

33.
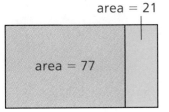

34.

area = 8n   area = 40

For Exercises 35–38, draw a figure to match each description. Then use the Distributive Property to write each area as a product and as a sum.

35. a 4-by-$(7 + 5)$ rectangle

36. an n-by-$(3 + 12)$ rectangle

37. a 3-by-$(2 + 4 + 2)$ rectangle

38. an n-by-$(n + 5)$ rectangle

39. Use the Distributive Property to write two equivalent expressions for the area of each figure below.

a.

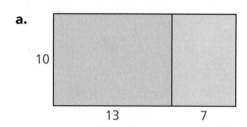

10

13   7

b.

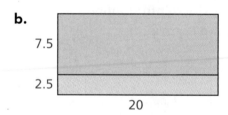

7.5

2.5

20

c. Compare the expressions for the two figures.

For Exercises 40–47, write $<$ **,** $>$ **, or** $=$ **to make each statement true.**

40. 2.4 ▨ 2.8

41. $\frac{5}{3}$ ▨ 1.666 . . .

42. 1.43 ▨ 1.296

43. $\frac{9}{2}$ ▨ 4.500

44. 5.62 ▨ 5.602

45. 0.32 ▨ 0.032

46. $3\frac{1}{4}$ ▨ $3\frac{1}{8}$

47. $\frac{343}{7}$ ▨ $\frac{343}{5}$

For Exercises 48–51, identify the coefficients. Then, determine how many terms are in each expression.

48. $4n + 5n + 3$

49. $6n + 4 + n + n$

50. $2n + 3 + 2n + 3$

51. $5(n + 3)$

52. Most states add a sales tax to the cost of nonfood purchases. Let p stand for the price of a purchase, t stand for the sales tax, and c for the total cost.

   a. What equation relates c, p, and t?

   For parts (b)–(d), suppose a state has a sales tax of 8%.

   b. What equation relates t and p?

   c. What equation relates c and p?

   d. Use the Distributive Property to write the equation relating c and p in a simpler equivalent form.

In Exercises 53–56, solve the given equations. Check your answers. Explain how you could find each solution with one or two arithmetic operations.

53. $x + 13.5 = 19$

54. $23 = x - 7$

55. $45x = 405$

56. $8x - 11 = 37$

57. Each equation below is a member of a fact family. Write other members of the fact families.

a. $8 + 7 = 15$

b. $7 \times 3 = 21$

c. $23 - 11 = 12$

d. $12 \div 4 = 3$

58. Show how fact families can be used to solve these equations.

a. $x + 7 = 15$

b. $7y = 21$

c. $w - 11 = 12$

d. $n \div 4 = 3.$

59. You are given the equation $y = 24 + 3x$.

a. Create a problem that can be represented by the equation.

b. Which of the points (60, 12) and (17, 75) lies on the graph of the equation?

c. Use the point that lies on the graph to make up a question that can be answered with the point.

60. You are given the equation $y = 120 + 4.5x$.

a. Create a problem that can be represented by the equation.

b. Which of these two points lies on the graph of the equation, (15, 180) or (8, 156)?

c. Use the point that lies on the graph to write an inequality that can be answered with the point.

In questions 61–64, solve each given inequality for x. Draw a number line graph of each solution.

61. $x + 13.5 < 19$

62. $23 > x - 7$

63. $45x < 405$

64. $8x > 48$

Extensions

65. In planning for a dance, the student government came up with these figures for income and costs.

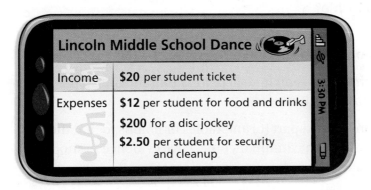

a. Write an equation that relates income I to the number of tickets sold for the dance n.

b. Write an equation that relates food and drink costs F to the number of tickets sold for the dance n.

c. Write an equation that relates the disc jockey fee D to the number of tickets sold for the dance n.

d. Write an equation that relates security and cleanup staff cost S to the number of tickets sold for the dance n.

e. Jamal and Sophie came up with two expressions for the relationship between profit P and number n of tickets sold.

> Jamal's Rule: $P = 20n - (12n + 200 + 2.5n)$
>
> Sophie's Rule: $P = 20n - 12n - 200 - 2.50n$

Are these equations correct models for the relationship between profit and number of customers? How do you know?

f. What simpler expression can be used to calculate profit for any number of tickets sold? Explain how you know that your answer is correct.

66. While planning their tour, the Ocean Bike Tours partners came up with an equation relating the number n of riders to the price p of the tour. The equation was $n = 50 - 0.10p$.

    a. How does the number of riders change as the price per rider increases? How is that pattern shown in a table and a graph of the relationship?

    b. Explain how the relationship between tour income I and tour price p can be expressed with the equation $I = (50 - 0.10p)p$.

    c. Show how the expression for calculating tour income in part (b) is equivalent to $50p - 0.10p^2$.

    d. Use the expression in part (c) and tables or graphs to find the tour price that will give maximum income. Give evidence to support your conclusion.

67. To get publicity for their Ocean Bike Tours business, the partners held a 30-mile bike race.

    • They gave riders under age 14 a half-hour head start.

    • The leading young riders rode at a steady speed of 12 miles per hour for the first half hour. Then, they rode 10 miles per hour for the rest of the race.

    • When the older riders started, the leading older riders went at a steady speed of 15 miles per hour.

    a. Write an equation that gives the distance d covered by the leading under-14 rider in t hours.

    b. Write an equation that gives the distance d covered by the leading older riders in t hours after the under-14 riders start.

    c. Use the equations from parts (a) and (b) to make a table and a graph comparing the progress of the two groups of riders.

    d. Write an equation for the time when the leading older riders catch up to the leading under-14 riders. Then solve it.

    e. Will the older riders catch up to the younger riders before the end of the 30-mile race? Explain how your answer is shown in the table and in the graph.

68. The managers of Wild World Amusement Park had an idea for changing the bonus card offered to park customers. Instead of giving 100 bonus points and charging 6 points per ride, they would give 150 bonus points and charge 12 points per ride. They thought that the card offering 150 bonus points would seem like a better deal.

    a. Which plan would actually offer the most rides?

    b. Write and solve an equation that finds the number of rides for which the two cards would leave the same number of points.

    c. For what numbers of rides would holders of the 150-point card have a greater number of points left?

69. A principal wants to send her top science students on a field trip to the state science center. The trip costs \$250 for a bus and driver, plus \$17.50 per student for food and admission.

    a. What is the cost of sending 30 students? 60 students?

    b. What equation shows how the total trip cost C depends on the number of students s who go on the trip?

    c. Write and solve an inequality that answers this question:

       How many students can go on the trip if the budget allows a maximum cost of \$1,000?

The Problems in this Investigation asked you to develop understanding and skill in writing equivalent algebraic expressions and solving equations. The following questions will help you summarize what you have learned.

Think about these questions. Discuss your ideas with other students and your teacher. Then write a summary of your findings in your notebook.

1. **What** does it mean to say that two expressions are equivalent? **How** can you test the equivalence of two expressions?

2. **What** does it mean to solve an equation. **What** strategies are available for solving equations?

3. **What** does it mean to solve an inequality? **What** will graphs of such solutions look like for inequalities in the form $ax > b$ and $a + x < b$? (Assume a and b are both positive numbers.)

4. **Describe** how expressions, equations, inequalities, and representations are used in this Unit. **How** are they related?

Common Core Mathematical Practices

As you worked on the Problems in this Investigation, you used prior knowledge to make sense of them. You also applied Mathematical Practices to solve the Problems. Think back over your work, the ways you thought about the Problems, and how you used Mathematical Practices.

Elena described her thoughts in the following way:

> In our group, we came up with several different ways to write the number of pieces needed to make the towers in Problem 4.1.
>
> Sally noticed that the first frame needs four pieces. Each frame after that only needs three more pieces. So, she wrote the expression $4 + 3(n - 1)$.
>
> Mitch made a table for the first 10 frames. He noticed a pattern relating the two variables in the table. The number of pieces is 3 times the frame number plus 1. So, he wrote $3n + 1$.
>
> We think that these two expressions are equivalent because the reasoning behind each made sense. We also substituted values for n into each expression and got the same value every time.

Common Core Standards for Mathematical Practice

MP3 Construct viable arguments and critique the reasoning of others.

- What other Mathematical Practices can you identify in Elena's reasoning?

- Describe a Mathematical Practice that you and your classmates used to solve a different Problem in this Investigation.

In this Unit, you studied some basic ideas of algebra. You learned ways to use those ideas to solve problems about variables and the patterns relating variables. In particular, you studied the following topics:

- Recognizing situations in which changes in variables are related in patterns

- Describing patterns of change shown in tables and graphs of data

- Constructing tables and graphs to display relationships between variables

- Using algebraic symbols to write equations relating variables

- Using tables, graphs, and equations to solve problems

Test Your Understanding and Skill

In the following Exercises, you will test your understanding of algebraic ideas and your skill in using algebraic techniques. You will consider how algebra is involved in shipping packages.

1. A shipping company offers two-day shipping of any package weighing as much as 2 pounds for $5 plus $0.01 per mile.

   a. Copy and complete the table.

   Two-Day Shipping Costs

Distance (mi)	100	200	300	400	500	1,000	1,500	2,000
Shipping Cost	■	■	■	■	■	■	■	■

   b. Describe the pattern by which the shipping cost increases as the shipping distance increases.

   c. Make a graph showing shipping charges for distances from 0 to 2,000 miles. Use appropriate labels and scales on the axes.

   d. Write an equation relating distance d in miles and shipping cost c in dollars.

   e. Use a graphing calculator and the equation from part (d) to check the graph you made in part (c).

   f. Use the table, graph, or equation to find the cost to ship a 1-pound package 450 miles.

   g. Use the table, graph, or equation to figure out how far you can ship a 2-pound package for $35.

   h. Write an inequality that describes the number of miles you can send a package for less than $15. Show the solution on a number line.

Look back at your work and answer the following questions.

2. What are the independent and dependent variables? How do you know?

3. How did you develop the equation relating distance and cost?

4. How did you choose scales for axes in the graph of the cost equation?

5. How could the relations in parts (f) and (g) be expressed as equations relating variables d and c?

6. How could the equations in Exercise 5 be solved by using the table or the graph? By reasoning with the symbolic forms alone?

A   **average speed** The number of miles per hour averaged over an entire trip. For instance, if you travel 140 miles in 2 hours, then the average speed is 70 miles per hour.

velocidad media El promedio del número de millas por hora durante un recorrido completo. Por ejemplo, si se recorren 140 millas en 2 horas, entonces la velocidad media es de 70 millas por hora.

C   **change** To become different. For example, temperatures rise and fall, prices increase and decrease, and so on. In mathematics, quantities that change are called *variables*.

cambiar Variar, volverse diferente. Por ejemplo, las temperaturas suben y bajan, los precios aumentan y se reducen, y así sucesivamente. En Matemáticas, las cantidades que cambian se llaman *variables*.

coefficient The numerical factor in any term of an expression.

coeficiente El factor numérico en cualquier término de una expresión.

compare *Academic Vocabulary*
To tell or show how two things are alike and different.

comparar *Vocabulario académico*
Decir o mostrar en qué se parecen y en qué se diferencian dos cosas.

related terms *analyze, relate*

términos relacionados *analizar, relacionar*

sample Two river rafting companies offer tours. The Rocky River Company charges $150 per group. Bailey's Rafting charges $37.50 per person. Compare these offers, and explain for which situations each offer is a better deal.

ejemplo Dos compañías de canotaje ofrecen excursiones. La Rocky River Company cobra $150 por grupo. La Bailey's Rafting cobra $37.50 por persona. Compara las dos ofertas y explica en qué situaciones una oferta es mejor que la otra.

Each choice would cost the same for 4 people since 4 x $37.50 = $150. If a group has fewer than 4 people, Bailey's is the better deal. If there are more than 4 people, Rocky River is the better deal.

I can also use a table to find a solution.

People	1	2	3	4	5
Rocky River	$150	$150	$150	$150	$150
Bailey's	$37.50	$75	$112.50	$150	$187.50

The cost is the same for 4 people.

Cada opción costaría lo mismo por 4 personas, ya que 4 x $37.50 = $150. Si el grupo tuviera menos de 4 personas, Bailey's es la mejor opción. Si tuviera más de 4 personas, Rocky River sería la mejor opción.

También puedo usar una tabla para hallar la solución.

Personas	1	2	3	4	5
Rocky River	$150	$150	$150	$150	$150
Bailey's	$37.50	$75	$112.50	$150	$187.50

El costo es el mismo por 4 personas.

coordinate graph A graphical representation of pairs of related numerical values that shows the relationship between two variables. It relates the independent variable (shown on the *x*-axis) and the dependent variable (shown on the *y*-axis).

gráfica de coordenadas Una representación gráfica de pares de valores numéricos relacionados que muestra la relación que existe entre dos variables. Dicha representación relaciona la variable independiente (que se muestra en el eje de las *x*) y la variable dependiente (que se muestra en el eje de las *y*).

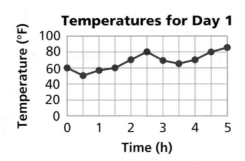

coordinate pair An ordered pair of numbers used to locate a point on a coordinate grid. The first number in a coordinate pair is the value for the *x*-coordinate, and the second number is the value for the *y*-coordinate. A coordinate pair for the graph shown above is (0, 60).

par de coordenadas Un par ordenado de números que se usa para localizar un punto en una gráfica de coordenadas. El primer número del par de coordenadas es el valor de la coordenada *x* y el segundo número es el valor de la coordenada *y*. Un par de coordenadas de la gráfica que se muestra arriba es (0, 60).

D **dependent variable** One of the two variables in a relationship. Its value depends upon or is determined by the other variable, called the *independent variable*. For example, the cost of trail mix (dependent variable) depends on how much you buy (independent variable).

variable dependiente Una de las dos variables de una relación. Su valor depende o está determinado por el valor de la otra variable llamada *variable independiente*. Por ejemplo, el costo de una mezcla de nueces y frutas secas (variable dependiente) depende de la cantidad de mezcla que compras (variable independiente).

E **equation** A rule containing variables that represents a mathematical relationship. An example is the formula for finding the area of a circle, $A = \pi r^2$.

ecuación Una regla que contiene variables que representa una relación matemática. Un ejemplo de ello es la fórmula para hallar el área de un círculo, $A = \pi r^2$.

equivalent expressions Expressions that represent the same quantity when the same number is substituted for the variable in each expression.

expresiones equivalentes Expresiones que representan la misma cantidad cuando el mismo número se sustituye por la variable en cada expresión.

expect Academic Vocabulary
To use theoretical or experimental data to anticipate a certain outcome.

esperar Vocabulario académico
Usar datos teóricos o experimentales para anticipar un resultado determinado.

related terms *anticipate, predict*

términos relacionados *anticipar, predecir*

sample Cynthia counted her sit-ups. Based on her data, how many sit-ups would you expect her to do in 40 seconds? Would you expect this pattern to continue indefinitely?

ejemplo Cynthia contó sus abdominales. Según sus datos, ¿cuántos abdominales esperas que haga en 40 segundos? ¿Esperas que este patrón continúe indefinidamente?

Seconds	10	20	30
Number of Sit Ups	6	12	18

Segundos	10	20	30
N° de abdominales	6	12	18

Cynthia's sit-ups increased by 6 every 10 seconds. Since 40 seconds is 10 more seconds than 30, I expect her to do 18 + 6 = 24 sit-ups.
I can also make a graph to represent this.

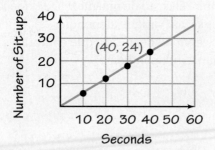

The graph shows 24 sit-ups at 40 seconds. I would not expect this pattern to continue because Cynthia will get tired and probably do fewer sit-ups.

Los abdominales que hace Cynthia aumentaron en 6 cada 10 segundos. Ya que 40 segundos son 10 segundos más que 30, espero que ella haga 18 + 6 = 24 abdominales.
También puedo hacer una gráfica para representar estos datos.

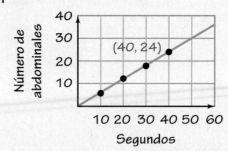

La gráfica muestra 24 abdominales en 40 segundos. No espero que este patrón continúe porque Cynthia se cansará y probablemente hará menos abdominales.

expression A mathematical phrase containing numbers, variables, and operation symbols.

expresión Una frase matemática que contiene números, variables y símbolos de operaciones.

English/Spanish Glossary

G **guess and check** A method of solving an equation that begins with a guess. The first guess is checked against the equation and corrected until an exact solution is reached.

suponer y comprobar Un método para resolver una ecuación que comienza con una suposición. La primera suposición se comprueba contra la ecuación y se corrige hasta que se llega a una solución exacta.

I **income** The amount of money taken in.

ingresos La cantidad de dinero que se gana.

independent variable One of the two variables in a relationship. Its value determines the value of the other variable, called the *dependent variable*. If you organize a bike tour, for example, the number of people who register to go (independent variable) determines the cost for renting bikes (dependent variable).

variable independiente Una de las dos variables relacionadas. Su valor determina el de la otra variable, llamada variable dependiente. Por ejemplo, si organizas un recorrido en bicicleta, el número de personas inscritas (variable independiente) determina el costo del alquiler de las bicicletas (variable dependiente).

O **order of operations**

A set of agreements or conventions for carrying out calculations with one or more operations, parentheses, or exponents.

1. Work within **parentheses**.
2. Write numbers written with **exponents** in standard form.
3. Do all **multiplication and division** in order from left to right.
4. Do all **addition and subtraction** in order from left to right.

orden de las operaciones Un conjunto de acuerdos o convenciones para llevar a cabo cálculos con más de una operación, paréntesis o exponentes.

1. Resolver lo que está entre **paréntesis**.
2. Escribir los números con **exponentes** en forma estándar.
3. **Multiplicar y dividir** en orden de izquierda a derecha.
4. **Sumar y dividir** en orden de izquierda a derecha.

P **pattern** A change that occurs in a predictable way. For example, the squares on a checkerboard form a pattern in which the colors of the squares alternate between red and black. The sequence of square numbers: 1, 4, 9, 16, . . . forms a pattern in which the numbers increase by the next odd number. That is, 4 is 3 more than 1, 9 is 5 more than 4, 16 is 7 more than 9, and so on.

patrón Un cambio que ocurre de manera predecible. Por ejemplo, los cuadrados del tablero de damas forman un patrón en el que los colores de los cuadrados se alternan entre el rojo y el negro. La secuencia de cuadrados de números: 1, 4, 9, 16, . . . forma un patrón en el que los números aumentan según la cifra del siguiente número impar. Es decir, 4 es 3 más que 1, 9 es 5 más que 4, 16 es 7 más que 9, y así sucesivamente.

profit The amount by which income is greater than expenses.

ganancias La cantidad en la cual los ingresos son mayores que los gastos.

R **rate of change** The amount of change in the dependent variable produced by a given change in the independent variable.

tasa de cambio La cantidad de cambio en la variable dependiente producida por un cambio dado en la variable independiente.

relationship An association between two or more variables. If one of the variables changes, the other variable may also change, and the change may be predictable.

relación Una asociación entre dos o más variables. Si una de las variables cambia, la otra variable también puede cambiar y dicho cambio puede ser predecible.

represent Academic Vocabulary
To stand for or take the place of something else. Symbols, equations, charts, and tables are often used to represent particular situations.

representar Vocabulario académico
Significar o tomar el lugar de algo más. Los símbolos, las ecuaciones, las gráficas y las tablas a menudo se usan para representar situaciones particulares.

related terms *symbolize, stand for*

términos relacionados *simbolizar, significar*

sample The Snowy Heights resort rents snowboards for $12 plus $3 for each hour. Write an equation to represent this situation. Explain what the variables and numbers in your equation represent.

ejemplo El centro de esquí Snowy Heights alquila tablas de snowboard por $12 más $3 por hora. Escribe una ecuación que represente esta situación. Explica lo que representan las variables y los números de tu ecuación.

My equation is $c = 12 + 3h$. The c represents the total cost. The 12 represents the initial charge for renting the snowboard. The h represents the number of hours rented, and the 3 represents the hourly charge.

Mi ecuación es $c = 12 + 3h$. La c representa el costo total. El 12 representa el cobro inicial por alquilar una tabla de snowboard. La h representa el número de horas de alquiler y el 3 representa el costo por hora.

rule A summary of a predictable relationship that tells how to find the value of a variable. A rule may be given in words or as an equation. For example, this rule relates time, rate, and distance: distance is equal to rate times time, or $d = rt$.

regla Un resumen de una relación predecible que indica cómo hallar el valor de una variable. Una regla se puede dar en palabras o como una ecuación. Por ejemplo, la siguiente regla relaciona tiempo, velocidad y distancia: la distancia es igual al producto de la velocidad y el tiempo, o sea $d = rt$.

scale A labeling scheme used on each of the axes on a coordinate grid.

escala Un esquema de rotulación que se usa en cada uno de los ejes de una gráfica de coordenadas.

solution of an equation The value or values of the variables that make an equation true.

solución de una ecuación El valor o valores de las variables que hacen que una ecuación sea verdadera.

solving an equation Finding the value or values of the variables that make an equation true.

resolver una ecuación Hallar el valor o valores de las variables que hacen que una ecuación sea verdadera.

table A list of values for two or more variables that shows the relationship between them. Tables often represent data made from observations, from experiments, or from a series of arithmetic operations. A table may show a pattern of change between two variables that can be used to predict values not in the table.

tabla Una lista de valores para dos o más variables que muestra la relación que existe entre ellas. Frecuentemente, las tablas representan datos provenientes de observaciones, experimentos o de una serie de operaciones aritméticas. Una tabla puede mostrar un patrón de cambio entre dos variables que se puede usar para predecir valores que no están en la tabla.

term A number, a variable, or the product of a number and a variable.

término Un número, una variable o el producto de un número y una variable.

variable A quantity that can change. Letters are often used as symbols to represent variables in rules or equations that describe patterns.

variable Una cantidad que puede cambiar. Suelen usarse letras como símbolos para representar las variables en las reglas o ecuaciones que describen patrones.

x-axis The number line that is horizontal on a coordinate grid.

eje de las x La recta numérica horizontal en una gráfica de coordenadas.

y-axis The number line that is vertical on a coordinate grid.

eje de las y La recta numérica vertical en una gráfica de coordenadas.

Index

Acknowledgments

Text

050 Tiger Missing Link Foundation

"*Typical Weights for Tiger Cubs*" from TIGERLINK.ORG. Used by permission.

Photographs

Photo locators denoted as follows: Top (T), Center (C), Bottom (B), Left (L), Right (R), Background (Bkgd)

002 David Maenza/Superstock; **003** Andre Jenny/Alamy; **014** Scott Neville/ AP Images; **017** (TL) Michele & Tom Grimm/Alamy, (TR) InterFoto/Travel/ Alamy; **019** SuperStock/Glow Images; **025** (BL, BR) GIPhotoStock/Science Source; **033** (BL) David Maenza/Superstock, (CR) Dallas and John Heaton/Free Agents Limited/Corbis; **048** Tony Donaldson/Icon SMI Tony Donaldson/Icon SMI Icon Sports Photos/Newscom; **090** Shirley Kilpatrick/Alamy.